How to Play the Federal Contractor Game to Win CAPTURE MANAGEMENT

By
David Browder
Ricki Henschel
and
David Kritzer

Cartoons by Joe Sutliff

Table of Contents

Why You Want to Read This Book 4

How to Read This Book 6

Section 1
So You're the Capture Manager. Now What? 8

Section 2
Everybody has a Role—and an Opinion 44

Section 3
Gathering What You Need 77

Section 4
How to Inspire the Client to Choose You 130

Section 5
Your Role Once the Solicitation Drops 195

Section 6
The Proposal is In—Don't Stop Now 207

Three Final Thoughts 214

Appendices 216

Why you want to read this book

The term "capture management" came about when companies found they couldn't win by writing a proposal based merely on the solicitation. Most solicitations lack real insights about what the customer wants, needs, or is being driven to do. Winning requires a dedicated effort from pursuit decision through solution development, pre-proposal preparation, proposal development, and post-submittal activities. This effort became known as the *capture phase* and the person designated to lead it, the *capture manager*.

Capture management can't be done by one person or by merely responding to the solicitation. It is a team sport. It requires knowing more about the customer, the opportunity, the requirements, the competitive environment, and your company. The capture manager must understand what needs to be accomplished, how to respond when things change (because they always do), and what it takes to get the most from everyone involved. Done well and enthusiastically, capture management is fun, challenging, and highly collaborative.

"She must have read the book."

Capture management is about gaining an information advantage and turning that advantage into a compelling proposal. You must develop your information advantage well *before the RFP/RFQ is released*. You need to hear the customer's exact words, which requires you have conversations with the customer. You then need to use their words to describe your solution. When you do, the customer hears themselves as they read your proposal.

Read this book to learn about structures, processes, and ways to think about capture management. This is based on our real-life experience—what works and what doesn't. But none of this is set in stone and we never let process get in the way of creativity and moving forward. What we present here are tools—use them and make them your own. This will help you respond to your real-world situations.

How to read this book

This is both a how-to and a reference book. You can go almost anywhere in the book (flip to any page) to gain information on how to do a good or better job at capture. Some redundancy and overlap have been purposely included so you always have context for what you're reading. For instance, we address aspects of "teaming" in many different places.

Who should read this book

1. People new to leading a capture or playing a major role for the first time.
2. Experienced capture managers looking for a tune-up.
3. Experienced capture managers who need a way of explaining the process to others.
4. Executives managing capture managers.

Using the cartoons

Humor goes a long way to being both memorable and powerful. So the authors and cartoonist grant permission for you to copy the cartoons to make your points with your colleagues.*

Customer and client

These words are used interchangeably in the book. This is to reflect the way you'll hear these words used at your company. When we say client or customer, we are not referring to one individual, but the various individuals within an organization who can influence the procurement and the selection of the winner. Even though an organization may not yet be a customer or client, we rarely hear them referred to as prospects, so have chosen not to use this word in the book.

*Distribution and republishing rights are not granted.

Playing the Contractor Game to Win

Section 1
So You're the Capture Manager. Now What?

"Do NOT make me come over there!"

Chapter 1
Stepping into Your Capture Shoes

Are you passionate about wanting to win? If you aren't ready to commit 110% to winning—find the door right away. Capture management takes focus, attention to detail, great desire, and time. It is likely this capture isn't your only job. You may be responsible for supporting other capture efforts or performing this capture in addition to your regular job. Regardless, you need to be willing to invest the effort needed to win.

You need to identify and get the resources necessary to successfully execute your capture plan. As well as having great organizational skills, you must be able to coordinate timelines (see Chapter 2), identify your company's value proposition (see Chapter 13), and ensure the benefits of your solution are articulated throughout the proposal. This means developing and communicating your win strategy (see Chapter 14) effectively to your management and the entire capture team. While doing this, you need to develop and prepare a solution that earns the customer's trust and positions your team to win.

Playing the Contractor Game to Win

"If it doesn't matter if you win or lose, then WIN, dammit!"

Expertise and experience

Successful capture managers—whether in-house managers or outside consultants—thrive on the challenge of putting together a winning team, possess the drive to see it through to proposal delivery, and the ego to believe they can do it better, faster, and cheaper. The best capture managers possess characteristics similar to great athletes. They possess an unrelenting will to win. They have a total commitment to preparedness by studying and knowing both the client and the competition. And they have demonstrated the ability to implement the right strategy and tactics necessary to win.

A capture effort can span months, even years. You must simultaneously ensure execution of the overall process while responding to day-to-day necessities. Your job is to ensure your team is progressing at least as quickly as the customer's acquisition. You don't want to be caught by surprise.

Focus

You must own the big picture. Visualize what a successful capture looks like from start to finish. Determine HOW your team can win and what must be done to do so. You'll go to sleep at night thinking about what to do next and wake up in the morning ready to execute.

Attention to detail

As you'll read later on, your capture manager role involves you with dozens of players from contracts and recruitment to top management and teaming partners. You'll be making commitments to all these people and tracking the commitments made by them.

Great desire

You face two major challenges. You'll be up against ferocious competitors—other companies who really want the work and are qualified to win it. You'll also be competing for your own corporate resources—money, subject matter experts, recruiters, contract specialists, etc. You must be the champion for winning this effort. Your corporate resources have plenty of work to do without helping you.

Ability and willingness to manage by influence

You'll be managing a project staff who do not report to you and have other demands on their time. You need to be able to work with varying types of individuals and get valuable contributions out of each person.

Time

Time to gather information. Time to think. Time to plan. Time to show up whenever and wherever you need to be. Time to work with your stakeholders. Time to ensure people are doing what they said they would do. Time to adjust what you know, who you know, and how everything fits together.

Understanding Your Role

Success depends on you understanding your role: Ensuring you have the right resources, they're deployed correctly, and barriers to their success are removed. It involves managing the entire process, being comfortable with priorities shifting as information becomes available, always knowing which items require the highest priority, and keeping the team working together toward the target you establish. This is a MADD position: Manager/Analyst/Diplomat/Decider.

Manager

You're responsible for positioning your company for a win and managing the resources invested in the capture. Your role is part business development and part operations. While you're focused on the win, your sponsors (corporate executives) expect you to also manage your capture as a project, using project management tools to enable them to clearly see what is required and when each major task needs to be completed. Know your budget if you are given one and manage against it. Some companies don't create budgets for capture. If you are not given a budget, discuss and obtain approval in advance of the costs you will have (e.g., personnel, travel, marketing) and make a budget so you can manage within it.

Managing also requires running your capture team by influence as the people on the capture team usually don't report to you. You must identify what contributions each person is capable of making, how best to work with them (e.g., who needs individual attention, who can run with tasks,) and then manage the team so you get high value out of each person. If anyone on the team is a distraction and not valuable, get them off the team.

So You're the Capture Manager

"I'm confident we'll make a great team, despite our obvious differences."

Analyst

People are looking to you for answers. Management wants to know how you intend to win, business development wants to know what customer calls to make, subject matter experts (SMEs) are questioning the customer's requirements, your proposal manager wants to know what the main themes are, and teammates want to know whether they can get a larger piece of the contract. Your role is to analyze information as it comes in (e.g., customer contact reports, intel on the competition, pricing data, inputs from subcontractors) and decide whether and how it impacts your capture (see Decider role).

Diplomat

This is potentially the most vital aspect of the capture manager role. As much as you'd like it to be at times, capture management is not a dictatorship and the various points of view can lead you to a stronger win position. Your responsibilities far exceed your direct authority and, because of the wide variety of people with whom you must deal, you will not be able to accomplish your tasks simply by ordering people to do your bidding.

As capture manager, you deal with a lot of people. You need to do it in a way to produce the maximum chance of winning and minimum chance of second guessing. Generally, you need to listen deeply and use dialogue and persuasion rather than ultimatums, whether dealing with executive management, your capture team, the review teams, teaming partners, or customers.

Decider

You need to make decisions to keep the capture effort progressing. You need to make decisions concerning teaming, pricing, and proposal strategies. You'll never have enough information, so be ready to determine when the information you have is sufficient to support a decision. There's always more information, but you need to know when it is worth the time and money to obtain—at some point it is not.

"Okay, call it in the air."

Leader

Above all else, you must make timely decisions. These decisions can be as trivial as whether to buy lunch for the team or as significant as whether to give up workshare to bring on a teammate. Your focus needs to be what will bring you the win. Once a decision is made, act on it and don't revisit it unless the circumstances have changed significantly. The capture team is looking to you to make decisions and then hold folks accountable for acting on those decisions. Nothing will undermine a capture team faster than not being able to get a decision or constantly changing decisions. When you do change a decision, you must explain clearly why you are making the change, and how the change makes it more likely you will win.

Always be learning

Curiosity may have killed the cat, but if you're not curious about the work, the people, and the opportunity, it will ultimately kill your PWIN (Probability of Win). Accept nothing as a given.

As you begin to understand the client's organization, the people who will be influencing the selection of the winner, and the work itself, you'll constantly find yourself asking more questions and looking for more answers. For example, you might want to know more about the funding stream, about the two subject matter experts (SMEs) who are fixated on creating a GOTS (Government Off The Shelf) solution instead of using a COTS (Commercial Off The Shelf) solution, about your competition's new hire or recent win, or about what the end consumers of your work are really trying to accomplish. Once you begin digging, the answers to these types of questions are rarely obvious or simple.

In Summary

Important to your success as capture manager is the desire to win...and you also need the abilities to:

- perform multiple roles;
- stay organized and focused in spite of changing priorities;
- analyze and respond to incoming information; and
- manage by influence up and down the chain.

Your role lasts from the time you're assigned until the contract is awarded.

Chapter 2
Your Capture is Your Baby. Take Charge. Manage It Well!

You have lots of responsibilities as capture manager. In addition to managing your capture team and working within your management structure, you must develop and maintain customer relationships, determine how to win, oversee execution of that strategy, guide development of your team's solutions, and make sure everything needed is completed correctly and at the right time. If this is making your head spin, you get it! To make sure all of this happens, you need to manage the capture as a project with a set of complex requirements, a budget, and a schedule. The following pages describe three tools we recommend you use to manage the capture effort: a capture calendar, a scorecard, and a dashboard. These tools allow you to clearly know and show what is required, when it is due, and who is responsible. They also provide the information you need to create a culture of information-sharing. How you do this is covered in Chapter 7.

"AHEM!"

Capture calendar

A capture calendar allows you to manage your capture activities. Capture management requires flexibility to respond to the fluidity of situations and the vagaries of customer actions. Capture management is not the same as project management—too little of the capture process is under your control for you to be able to accurately forecast the sequence, duration, resource requirements, and schedule constraints for each individual action. You need to resist management pressure to develop a detailed schedule in any project-type scheduling tool and then use that schedule to manage your capture. Explaining the lack of such a schedule does not indicate you are unwilling to implement a plan or provide management with adequate oversight. It simply acknowledges the reality of the ever-changing nature of capture. You must use other techniques to ensure you can track and control what needs to be done as well as give management visibility.

The capture calendar lets you identify the activities required for a successful capture (e.g., research, marketing campaign, solution development (technical, staffing, management), proposal development) and then manage the alignment of those activities with the customer's acquisition activities. This tool allows you to identify what you need to do, develop an estimate of the effort required for each activity, and control their execution.

The detail within the capture calendar depends on the complexity of the capture. It should lay out the capture plan clearly so everyone can see when things need to get done based on the customer's schedule. Each event on the calendar is associated with a part of your capture plan. For example, you can use different colors or other techniques to differentiate customer events from capture team events. You will then see when the customer is not keeping their schedule and how it impacts your capture activities. You can create more detailed schedules for specific capture activities, such as complex solution development, to complement and supplement the capture calendar.

The events on the capture calendar should be approved and managed by you. The activities associated with these events can be maintained by the lead for those areas (e.g., business developer, solution architect, recruiting lead, proposal manager). Your calendar will include:

- acquisition milestones, if you have them (e.g., industry day, draft solicitation release, final solicitation release, proposal due date, orals, contract award);
- meetings: customer meetings, teaming meetings, capture team meetings (recurring status meetings and ad hoc issue-oriented meetings), and senior-level meetings to keep management apprised;
- formal reviews (executive-level briefings to obtain and retain corporate support);
- research and analysis (e.g., on client, competition, stakeholders);
- contact plans (e.g., individual call plans, social media engagements, conferences/seminars/meetings);
- marketing/branding initiatives;
- strategy/solutioning sessions;
- Program and/or Project Manager and other Key Personnel (requirements, identification, selection, commitment);
- staffing (skills, knowledge, abilities, number, size);
- teaming (requirements, identification, selection, commitment); and
- pricing, including Price to Win (PTW) (see Chapter 16).

Using the capture calendar

A common technique is to reverse engineer and put down anything you know. For larger acquisitions this could be the client's advertised acquisition schedule (e.g., announcement, industry day, solicitation release, contract award). For smaller opportunities or within some agencies, you may just have an anticipated solicitation release, if that. Add other anticipated client milestones (e.g., draft solicitation, one-on-one/on-site visit, receipt of proposals, anticipated award date).

Now identify what events and activities associated with your capture plan you need to complete and when they need to occur to fully implement your win strategy. Use the client's milestones as opportunities to confirm your capture efforts are proceeding correctly. Your capture plan should define what tasks you expect to complete prior to each milestone. Essentially, you're back-scheduling to ensure you're able to have as many client touches as possible, interactions with stakeholders, and discussions with competition and potential teaming partners before the "cone of silence" * drops and your capture focus narrows. Events on the calendar provide prospective for the timing of capture activities (e.g., solutioning, teaming, competitive analysis).

Use whatever tool (e.g., spreadsheet, text table, project planning tool) allows you to easily modify, add, and depict the timing of capture events. Then use the calendar to make sure everyone on your team is aware of when you expect their activities to occur. Add details for the upcoming month to identify the 2-3 focus areas you view as critical to the win and provide more details about other events upcoming. Usually, customer events or formal reviews identify when capture events need to be completed. Highlight the things you complete so you can see immediately what still needs to be done. Your capture calendar provides a visual map of your capture plan, including the steps to be taken and the timetable for their completion.

* "Cone of silence" refers to the blackout period during which only formal written communication is allowed. Generally, the customer is not allowed to have conversations with potential offerors about the opportunity or solicitation during this period.

Benefits of the capture calendar

A capture calendar can be a valuable tool in the overall process, whereas trying to use a list to track all the details needed to manage an entire capture effort is a fool's errand. There are many reasons for this. For example, government captures often extend over several months and can last years. You can only control a limited portion of what may happen. Even high-level schedules can become unwieldly and difficult to maintain. Your capture calendar enables you to highlight the relationship between the elements of your capture plan and the client's acquisition schedule. From the moment you start the capture effort, your capture calendar facilitates discussions about schedules, objectives, and budget. It helps you achieve buy-in from everyone involved. It allows each person to see when and how they will be needed, and to plan their individual capture activities. It allows you to continually reassess your focus and adjust based on:

- evolving/changing client priorities, personnel, and policies;
- changes to the acquisition schedule;
- what is influencing the influencers; and
- where you are and where your competition is in relation to positioning for the win—solution, staff, etc.

For example, the calendar should include an internal review to finalize what will be presented to the client, followed by a client meeting to vet a portion of your solution. This means you should see solutioning meetings scheduled during the period preceding the internal review. If you don't, the calendar shows the obvious disconnect to address. Visual displays are often more insightful than your words.

Example Calendar, mid-May, highlighting what has been done.

	May	June	July
Client communication	Work call plans—talk to contracting officer	Work call plans June 10th: XYZ conference; talk to client about ZZZ	Work call plans
Solutioning (tech)	May 25th: solutioning meeting on ZZZ	June 12th: discussion of client reactions	
Staffing	May 10th: finalize contingent hiring of ZZZ expert May 10th and 25th: HR/recruiting review	Finalize PM and 2 key SMEs	Finalize staffing
Teaming	Who do we want to talk to at XYZ conf	Finalize team	
Pricing		First cut at PTW	
Research	Obtain more current competitor pricing		
Internal meetings	Weekly core meetings Figure out who we want to bump into at XYZ conference and get everyone prepared	Weekly core meetings Hot wash of conference Competitive analysis	Weekly core meetings
Marketing	Work with marketing to prep for XYZ conference		
Formal internal briefs	May 30th	June 27th	July 25th

Scorecard and dashboard (overview of your capture plan)

In addition to the capture calendar, we recommend you use the combination of a scorecard and dashboard to keep your capture team informed about how well everyone is doing. One or more dashboards are a highly effective way to summarize and present the key performance indicator (KPIs) data. The scorecard provides the detail behind the dashboard. The dashboard provides everyone on the team with a snapshot of the status at the current time and is extremely useful for formal reviews (see Chapter 3). The scorecard is based on KPIs for your capture effort. These metrics provide visibility above the day-to-day activity level and allow you to assess how well you're doing against your capture plan.

The team scorecard and dashboard should be readily available to the entire capture team. Together they provide a summary and snapshot of the status at a point in time. The combination of the two allows everyone to have a quick visual on where the capture is in terms of progress, or lack thereof, and can motivate your team.

The next section provides examples of scorecards and dashboards.

Scorecard

A scorecard is an easy way to collect and consolidate KPI data. Use it to assess the status of key elements of your capture plan. The sample scorecard below provides examples of the areas you want to track. Use a 1-to-5 scoring method, or whatever other scoring method may be appropriate for your company as long as it covers the following four levels: great, good, neutral, needs help. Scores should reflect where you are relative to where you need to be based on the maturity of your customer's acquisition. Be honest—you need to accurately reflect your status. Use low scores (some 1s, 2s, and 3s) to reflect where additional resources or work may be needed. Be prepared to describe the effort required to get the score to a winning level (4s and 5s). Color-coding your numbers also gives a quick snapshot of where you stand. Update the scorecard at least monthly and use it as the basis for your presentation as part of each formal review.

Scorecard	Score (1-5: low to high)			
Key Capture Plan Elements	Date:	Date:	Date:	Date:
Strategic Corporate Fit				
Knowledge of the Acquisition Strategy				
Current Customer Relationship(s)				
Knowledge of the Evaluators				
Knowledge of the Customer Needs (as articulated by the customer)				
Knowledge of the "as is" environment (technical)				
Technical Solution (as perceived by the customer)				
Teaming Strategy				
Program Manager (known and trusted by the customer)				
Key Personnel and Staffing (who we need to fill substantive requirements, meet certification requirements, or be known by the customer)				
Identified Differentiators (based on customer needs)				
Knowledge of Competition and Ability to Ghost Them				
Past Performance (with customer and/or highly relevant experience)				
Pricing/Cost Competitive (know competition; pricing strategy to beat them)				
Conflicts of Interest				
Corporate Risk (minimize execution risk)				
Capture and Proposal Resources				
FILL IN OTHER SPECIFICS BASED ON THIS OPPORTUNITY				
TOTAL SCORE				

Dashboard

Dashboards (one or more) are a highly effective way to summarize and present the KPI data from the scorecard. We recommend using colors or other visual cues to draw attention to the items needing attention. The sample below is an example of an executive dashboard you can use during formal reviews. You can use a dashboard to aggregate and summarize the information from the scorecard in an easy-to-understand format. It draws attention to the areas you want to discuss in more detail and helps drive tactical and strategic decisions.

You can use a slightly more detailed dashboard to keep the capture team aware of the various aspects of the capture effort. It and the scorecard help them understand how their efforts contribute to the overall effort and whether specific efforts are making appropriate progress.

Sample Dashboard

Capture Area	Current Score	Trend
Customer	Excellent Progress	↑
Requirements	Good Progress	
Solution	Needs Attention	↓
Teaming	Critical	↓
Competition	Excellent Progress	

Legend

‖‖‖‖‖	Excellent Progress		Needs Attention
≡≡≡≡	Good Progress		Critical

Chapter 3
Formal Reviews

Gate, step, stage review—whatever your company calls it, reviewing where you are at any given time is an essential part of the capture process. These reviews are your opportunity to discuss what you need to win and share challenges. Each review is essentially a go/no-go decision based on your progress measured against your win strategy and the status of the acquisition. Obtaining and then maintaining senior management buy-in is important to your decision-making, allowing you to check your thought process on the project. Getting input from good minds not engaged in the capture can prevent your developing tunnel vision. Remember senior management needs to approve risk and return on investment, as well as consider your ability to win and decide on resource allocation. Hiding issues will come back to bite you! The kinds of information you'll need for these formal reviews are discussed later in this chapter.

Each company has its own review process. If your company doesn't have one, implement one.

"I think it's important that we ackowledge how this reflects on everyone's performance this year."

Who should attend

Formal reviews allow you to lay out where you are and what you need to win. The right people need to be present so you can get the resources you need. Formal reviews also enable you to hear, firsthand, from those who have issues with the opportunity or your current win strategy.

So who attends a formal review? (Be aware there are often attendees who cannot contribute much!) Your job is to make sure the people who need to be there are there. In large companies there is usually a list of those who routinely get invited to these reviews, and your job is to add the right folks, who may or may not be regulars.

Depending on your capture, the necessary attendees include:
- the decision authority (e.g., senior management);
- the business line owner of the opportunity;
- the individual(s) who best know(s) the client;
- your lead technical SME(s);
- the individual who is working "price to win";
- recruiting personnel;
- the likely proposal manager; and
- contracts staff.

If your company does not have a set list to which you add, make sure to invite those C suites and/or senior managers who can determine the success or failure of your capture. Also invite subject matter experts who may not be engaged in the capture and who have important experience, knowledge, and/or relationships.

Questions to answer at a formal review

Based on a sample process including four reviews, we are providing representative questions you need to be able to answer. The exact number of reviews you have isn't important. What is important is making sure your capture efforts are leading to answers to these questions, and the answers are maturing at a rate commensurate with the acquisition life cycle. As the acquisition matures, you have more questions to answer (see Chapter 7) and your answers need to be more specific.

Use the scorecard and dashboard (see Chapter 2) to track your progress in answering these questions. You may not have all the information to respond to the questions; your scores on your capture dashboard should reflect what you have been able to accomplish. Generally, you'll be expected to update previous answers at each review and your score should reflect that progress. The further into the process, the greater the detail required in answering these questions and showing how the win strategy is evolving. The primary question is always "How will you WIN?".

So You're the Capture Manager

"You know, some people would be content with just asking if he was a vegetarian."

Formal Review 1

This review occurs when management first decides to enter into capture—to spend resources on positioning for the win. Usually this is when the capture manager is assigned. You should get senior management buy-in; and set a schedule for less formal check-ins, reports, and follow-on formal reviews. Except for the first two areas listed below, you may not have all of the answers, but you need to acknowledge what you know, what you don't know, and how you plan to gain knowledge quickly.

- Is the opportunity real?
  - How well has the customer identified their requirements?
  - Does the customer have a budget to address these requirements?
  - Is it work you know how to do?
- Why do you want this work?
  - How does it fit your company's business strategy?
  - What value does the new contract bring?
- What is your win strategy (see Chapter 14)?
  - How does it get you to a win?
  - What aspect is of greatest concern right now?
  - What do you need to be able to execute it?

- Who is the client?
  - Is this an existing client?
  - If so, how does the client view us (positive, neutral or negative)? Identify current issues.
  - If not, explain *how we will get the client to know and want us.*
  - How have you structured your call plan (see Chapter 15) to obtain the information you need?
  - How do the relationships your team has (or does not have) affect your call plan?
- Do you know who is influencing the acquisition?
  - Who's driving the acquisition in the client organization?
  - Who's influencing the acquisition strategy?
  - What's the schedule for your call plan across all organizations involved in the acquisition?
- Who is your competition?
  - Is there an incumbent?
  - What companies are expressing interest?
  - Is there a particularly well-positioned competitor? Why and how?

Formal Review 2

Present your rationale for continuing, describe your progress (or lack thereof) at implementing your win strategy, present your initial win theme, and discuss the results of your competitive analysis. It's important to get input from senior management not engaged in the capture to make sure you're not missing major elements necessary to the win.

- What progress have you made on your call plan (see Chapter 15)?
- What new information do you have on your client?
- What new information do you have on your competition (e.g., hires, wins, awards)?
- What do we know about the client's acquisition strategy and history (e.g., through experience, FOIA [Freedom of Information Act] requests)?
  - What preferences has the customer expressed regarding potential solutions?
  - What opportunities are there to influence the acquisition (e.g., the way the requirements are expressed, the type of procurement, the evaluation criteria)?
  - What are the potential issues (technical, political, pricing)?
  - What pricing strategies have won before for this type of acquisition?
- What type of acquisition is it?
  - Is it a single or multiple award?
  - What type of contract is it?

- What is the period of performance?
  - Is the period of performance realistic?
  - Is there anything unique about the period of performance (e.g., base contract and option periods)?
  - Can you win alone or do you need teammates?
- Why are you including teammates?
  - To fill gaps (e.g., technical, past performance, customer insight)?
  - To meet small or disadvantaged business requirements?
  - To satisfy customer desires?
  - How are you identifying and vetting subcontractors (subs)?
- Who is your competition?
  - What does the competition tell you about the opportunity?
  - What's the schedule for competitive reviews?
  - Where do you stand in comparison with the competition?
- Do your themes resonate with the customer?
  - Why do you think the customer will respond well to your win themes (see Chapter 14)?
  - How will your win themes manifest themselves in your solution?
  - How will your win themes convince the customer your offer is the best?

Formal Review 3

Present an update of where you are—based on new information and progress to date (or lack thereof). Identify how your solution and price-to-win respond to your competitive analysis. Review previous answers about how you win, any gaps, any concerns, and any red flags. What do you want/need to change?

- What progress have you made on your call plan?
- What new information do you have on your client?
    - What new information do you have on your competition (e.g., hires, wins, awards)
    - Has the customer provided a draft of the solicitation (all or portions)?
    - How does the draft solicitation affect your win strategy?
- What concerns do you have about it (e.g., does the language favor the incumbent or another competitor? Are there requirements you can't meet?)
    - What areas provide you with an advantage?
- Have you completed your competitive analysis?
    - What did it tell you about the acquisition?
    - How did it affect your win strategy?
- Have you identified your solution?
    - Does your solution meet the customer's requirements within the established budget?

- What features of your solution exceed the customer's requirements/expectations?
- What features of your solution differentiate you from your competition?
* Have you identified key personnel?
  - Have you identified a PM and key staff?
  - Are they known, liked, and trusted by the client? Explain.
  - If not, explain how you intend to make them known and trusted?
  - Do the PM and key staff have experience consistent with your proposed solution?
* Have you identified your PTW (see Chapter 16)
  - Why do you think it is a winning price?
  - Do your solution and key personnel allow you to meet the PTW?
  - Is your company willing to propose that price?
* What is the estimated total contract value?
  - What's the total estimated revenue?
  - What portion of the revenue is from subcontracts or other direct costs?
  - What is the anticipated profit as a percentage of total revenue?

Formal Review 4

Present a further update of where you are—based on the solicitation, using the full list of questions and answers from the previous formal reviews to indicate how you intend to win, any gaps, any concerns, any red flags. Other questions to answer are:

- What progress have you made on your call plan?
- What new information do you have on your client?
- What new information do you have on your competition (e.g., hires, wins, awards)
- Are there any surprises in the final solicitation?
  - Are you able to tell who within the customer organization had the greatest influence?
  - Are there any indications you or the competition affected the solicitation?
  - Is there any reason to revisit the bid/no-bid decision?
- Does the solicitation require you to make changes in your proposed solution?
  - Does your solution meet the customer's requirements within the established budget?
  - Which evaluation criteria allow features of your solution to score well?
  - Which evaluation criteria require you to modify your solution to differentiate you from your competition?

- How do the evaluation criteria affect your key personnel?
    - Does the solicitation require key personnel?
    - How well will your PM and key staff score against the evaluation criteria?
    - What key personnel changes, if any, do you need to make?
- How do the evaluation criteria effect your PTW?
    - How important is price to the selection of the winner?
    - How's price evaluated (e.g., did the Government provide an evaluation model)?
    - Do you need to adjust your price?

Playing the Contractor Game to Win

Section 2
Everybody's Got
a Role—and an Opinion

"Exactly WHAT is your objection to having a bird feeder in the executove lunchroom?"

Chapter 4
Becoming a
Relationship Expert

Too often the relationship piece of capture management gets short shrift. You need to maintain relationships within your company—with your management and capture teams—as well as relationships between you and your customers and other stakeholders. The frequent lack of emphasis on this element is unfortunate because as the capture manager, you are responsible for managing so many different relationships. In addition to managing the capture team, you need to:

- avoid surprises;
- keep executive management informed and aware of any support you need;
- use both formal reviews and have regular check-ins;
- identify who you need on your capture and review teams;
- ensure cooperation among teaming partners from initiation, during the proposal phase, and through the award; and
- manage the customer relationship, including what contacts are made and who makes them.

For team members and hires, you need to continue to hand hold while working to foster relationships with the proposed Program Manager, other appropriate members of the proposed project management, and other members of your capture team.

Playing the Contractor Game to Win

"By the power vested in me by the Acquisition Team, I pronounce you Technical and Financial proposal managers. You may kiss your personal time goodbye."

Executive management

In dealing with your company's executive management, your objective is to secure their support. This support often involves:

- assigning personnel they consider too valuable or over-committed to make available for the capture;
- providing a budget exceeding what they want to spend;
- relinquishing workshare they don't want to give up; and
- reducing the proposed price to the point of discomfort.

Be aware of how they might respond and be prepared. Before asking for any type of support, make sure you understand what you want. Remember the executive is trading off your request against other demands for attention, resources, and support. Provide a clear, unemotional connection between what you are asking for and its contribution to winning. Make sure your presentation includes a realistic assessment of what it will take to win and accept nothing less. You're not simply trying to win an argument; you're trying to convince them of the logic behind your request.

Real-life example of what executive support can do

We had to convince senior management to spend on an advertising campaign to portray the company as one of the "big boys," as the client was very clear there would be a set number of spots available, and they wanted companies with depth and breadth. At the time, this was not how we were seen. We took out billboard ads on mass transit near the client offices, along with radio ads. We wanted to convince the client we were comparable to our competition, with whom they already viewed as deep and broad. It worked!

Everyone Has A Role

Review teams

As the capture manager, you want to use review teams to provide a perspective from outside your capture team on your proposed solution, value propositions (see Chapter 13), and competition. Ideally, you want some of the people who participated in early solution reviews, client discussions, and competition assessments to also participate in formal reviews of the actual proposal. During reviews before the RFP drops, you will want to select participants according to the scope of the specific review, as you may be working only one aspect of the solution or pricing or be conducting a competitive analysis. If you are lucky, you will have a choice of who is on the review teams. Frequently, you're asked to include senior personnel from your company and your teammates. Look for a combination of talents, some who are technical, some who are not. Try to include at least one person familiar with the specific opportunity. If someone is known to provide good insights or specific knowledge, it is good practice to include them even if they are not familiar with the specific opportunity. If possible, try to include retired members of the customer or incumbent organization. You need people who can identify:

- your weaknesses and strengths;
- your competition's weaknesses and strengths;
- credible solutions;
- exaggerated claims;
- unsupported claims;
- incomplete solutions; and
- relationship-building opportunities.

Playing the Contractor Game to Win

Getting what you need from this diverse group requires real diplomacy. To obtain as much constructive input from them as possible, remind reviewers their role is to provide input, not simply to criticize. Set expectations in terms of their preparation and participation. If they do not meet your expectations, try not to include them in future reviews. If they, or their company insist on their participation, find someone who can help them understand what the capture team needs. Usually, they wouldn't be a candidate if they didn't bring a particular insight. You must extract what is useful to get to the win. Be careful to avoid letting anyone distract the capture team.

Teaming partners

Typically, your early capture efforts involve identifying what your preferred team looks like and courting the best teaming partners. Even though teaming arrangements can't be finalized until the government makes their decisions about the contract vehicle and who is eligible to bid as prime (e.g., whether the procurement is a set aside), you should still attempt to gain commitments to team. Structure the teaming agreement to confirm the commitment and establish the basis for roles.

Always identify options in case your desired team isn't possible. Continually look for companies that significantly improve your win probability based on a gap (political, technical, socioeconomic) you're filling. During this phase, you or members of your capture team are convincing representatives from those companies that your company has the best chance to win, and why having them on your team improves the win probability (P,win).

Occasionally, business development has made commitments to team with other companies before you joined the capture. Some of these may not be the best companies to execute your win strategy. Try to determine whether these companies are essential to winning and what options you have. Be sure to vet them with the client—are these potential teaming partners known or unknown? Are they liked, trusted, and respected? What else does the client know about them?

Teaming partners may be companies with which you team often and have a long-term relationship. Sometimes you may need to team with a company with which you routinely compete. Rightfully, both your company and this frequent competitor approach these negotiations with caution. At the same time, be aware the other company may be considering other options, including priming or joining another team. You need to be cognizant of the potential for a competitor to extract information from you by talking and talking. They also may begin negotiations and then let them drag on to delay your teaming decisions. You must read body language (even over video chat) and question time lags and delays when they impact your capture timeline.

As capture manager, you need to help management on both sides to see the value in teaming and determine whether an agreement can be reached that will both maximize the likelihood of winning and make good business sense for both sides. A bad deal for either side will eventually jeopardize the capture, and often at the worst possible time. (See Chapter 9, Picking the Right Teammates.)

Everyone Has A Role

The customer

As the capture manager, you manage the customer relationships related to this opportunity. You may interface directly with the customer or coach others who have those relationships. Whoever from your capture team meets directly with the customer organization must recognize they are the ambassador for your team. In this role, their goal is to get the customer interested in your team, your solution, as the best answer to their problem(s). Therefore, we use Call Plans (See Call Plan Support in Chapter 5). This means you must learn as much as you can about the customer, the specific opportunity, and criteria for selecting a winner. You then must translate your team's capabilities and ideas into material the customer finds relevant to their needs and their basis for selection. Often this requires you to work indirectly, through surrogates (e.g., consultants, influencers, subject matter experts) who can provide the insights you need.

"I'll know which one it is when I see it."

Chapter 5
Getting What You Need from Your Capture Team

Getting your capture team fully engaged and working together is potentially the hardest part of capture management. Your capture team is often composed of people for whom supporting the capture is not their primary work assignment. They have other jobs (with real bosses), coming from multiple organizations. They will be supporting the capture on a part-time basis. Often, they don't work for you. Your capture is not their top priority.

At the early stage of capture, you need to worry less about the budget and specific assignments and concentrate instead on getting the right personnel. Your role is to quickly determine who the key contributors are to get to the win and get them working together. Then you need to get them as enthused about the opportunity as you are. This requires strong emotional intelligence and interpersonal skills (e.g., active listening, collaboration, problem solving, conflict resolution, empathy). We've included in the appendices an extensive list of books on emotional intelligence, interpersonal intelligence, and conflict resolution. We recommend you use these resources to further strengthen your skills.

Everyone Has A Role

"Okay, ready to make history?"

Your capture team

In managing your team, your focus is helping everyone to give the capture their best efforts. The capture team requires many types of support: SMEs, generalists, pricing, PTW, marketing, contracts, and recruiting. Also a Proposal Manager, if you're fortunate enough to have one. As Capture Manager, you're focused on the win. As we said before, many on your team may be working on other, billable projects and your capture is not their highest priority. You must use whatever influence you have to get their time commitment and buy-in.

You need to get the Capture Team to function as a team. This is not a hero sport—it's a team sport. Your team includes a range of personalities, from intimidators to those easily intimidated. Not everyone grasps information at the same rate or in the same manner. And there can be important members who must float in and out based on their availability. You must identify what contributions you need from each person and how best to get those from them.

Ask each team member how they prefer to communicate—phone, email, text, video conferencing—and if there are times that are never good for them. Showing you are cognizant of individual preferences and needs, and respecting them, matters.

Occasionally, group meetings are important to make sure your core capture team functions as a team. Clear agendas, objectives, and expectations for and from each meeting ensure they are productive. Use these meetings only as necessary. Also, some of your team may require one-on-one time with you. Give them that time. Take the time to be human—check in with team members and ask how they are doing.

Also, use your emotional intelligence to determine if someone is overly stressed or responding or acting in an unexpected manner—check in with them. Kindness goes a long way in developing a team.

And remember, not everyone may be worth the effort required, and you can't allow yourself to be consumed by one or two needy individuals. If someone is requiring more time or energy than their contribution is worth, thank them for their contributions to date and tell them you'll reconnect if their help is needed in the future. Minimize the turmoil associated with any individual's departure. At the same time, don't let them talk you into having them remain on the capture team and negatively impacting the overall effort.

Playing the Contractor Game to Win

How to work with your SMEs

Be creative in terms of how you engage your SMEs. Do not waste their time or yours. Make sure each meeting is well-planned with clearly defined outcomes. Do not be afraid to escalate issues of the lack of availability of a member of the capture team, if they can't seem to shake loose the time you need from them.

The next few pages identify a few potential scenarios you, as the capture manager, may face as you work with members of your capture team. Differences of opinion among team members will inevitably occur, regardless of whether this is a major recompete, a takeaway from the competition, or a new piece of work.

Everyone Has A Role

"Keep looking. There are forty-seven more after this one."

Playing the Contractor Game to Win

Scenario #1

You have smart and highly passionate SMEs and they have developed an amazing solution—except the price is higher than the customer's anticipated budget. This is a loser. No matter how great your solution, don't knowingly submit a proposal that exceeds the customer's budget. Realize the customer has invested time and energy in their acquisition strategy including establishing their budget.

If you're convinced there are no solutions available to meet the customer's requirements within the anticipated budget, here are four options.

Try to Change Your Solution
You must get your solutioning team to develop solutions executable within this customer's budget. This is where you need to draw on your understanding of what the customer really wants from this contract and the requirements on which they are willing to compromise. Force the SMEs to explain why they're recommending each element of the solution. Ask them what alternative approaches they considered and whether any of those would produce a compliant outcome at a lower cost. Ask them to explain how they would do the work differently if they were only going to meet the requirements at the lowest possible cost. Ask them to identify any deliverables they included for which there isn't a requirement.

Try to Change the Requirements
If you're early in the acquisition process, you may be able to influence the way in which the requirements are stated. You must identify the specific requirements causing all potential solutions to exceed the budget. Then offer alternative language that allows the customer to meet their mission requirements within the budget and without restricting competition. This usually means being less prescriptive and permitting offerors to make tradeoffs. Tradeoffs could include higher costs up front with lower costs in the out years.

Try to Change the Budget
This option has a low probability of success UNLESS you're early enough in the acquisition planning process to engage with the customer and influence the budget. This requires helping the customer understand why their budget is insufficient and providing them with objective and impartial information they can use to defend a budget change before the solicitation is released. Be aware, this only works when you can validate the other options will not solve their problem and they will come out with hero status based on the program. The client is highly unlikely to push for a budget change if none of the other potential offerors are indicating the budget is inadequate and the client believes one or more of your competitors' solutions will solve their problem(s).

Make a No-Bid Decision
If your solutioning team can't identify an affordable solution (one within the customer's budget), you'd be wasting your company's money to continue with the capture. Advise your management of the reason for your recommendation and the alternatives you considered. If they agree, notify the customer. Let the customer know why you decided not to bid. This may influence the acquisition authority's decision about changing the budget or the requirements.

Playing the Contractor Game to Win

Scenario #2

You have a great solution and great people to offer— except your SMEs are not comfortable talking with the customer. This is your time to guide and mentor. You need to spend time and figure out ways for SMEs to be more comfortable meeting with the customer.

There are multiple ways to tackle this.

- Think about how you can get them to meet. Will your SMEs be presenting a paper or be serving on a panel at a conference? Is your SME a member of a professional association, technical forum, or user group in which members of the customer organization are engaged? If they can use these connections to develop relationships with people within the customer organization, arranging for them to meet becomes easier.
- Find out what makes them uncomfortable—this is one of many places where curiosity and caring about people will serve you well. If you find out what the barriers are, you may be able to address them.
- Get your SME(s) to talk to you about their work and their ideas, then ask them why they are nervous about having the same conversation with the client—keep asking questions.
- Role play until they are comfortable discussing the solution with others.

Role playing can help them understand you aren't asking them to sell something. You merely want them to engage the customer in a conversation about how best to solve the customer's problems. You want them in the room to describe how we think the problem can be solved and to hear firsthand the customer's feedback.

Don't feel you always need to do this yourself. Identify individuals (other SMEs who are comfortable, consultants) to help.

"Stop putting yourself in a box and learn to communicate."

Scenario #3

Your team has great ideas—except they are not spending the time and energy required to flesh them out. This significantly limits your ability to vet the ideas within the customer organization and may result in an incomplete solution in the proposal.

Try one-on-one conversations with your lead SMEs. Make sure they understand the level of detail required and are willing to commit to providing a complete solution. Make sure they understand great ideas aren't enough. Then have them help you make it clear to the entire solutioning team they will not win unless they invest the energy necessary to flesh out their ideas.

Try breaking the solutioning team into smaller teams (even one or two people). Assign each team one of the ideas (or even part of it) and ask them to describe how they would implement it on this contract. Have them make a succinct presentation on their work to the larger solutioning team. Have the total solutioning team vote on each of the ideas to identify which are worthy of further consideration. Using online survey tools makes the voting more interesting, allows anonymous voting, and quickly gets you the results. This capability is contained in many collaboration tools. Repeat the process as needed until the ideas become detailed and all the requirements are addressed.

If this doesn't work, escalate the issue—be clear on why this is important to maximizing the team's win potential. Consider making changes in the composition of your solutioning team.

Everyone Has A Role

"Go in first and see if they're friendly."

How to work with your business development (BD) person or group

As companies grow, they often begin to divide responsibilities and assign them to separate people. If your company has reached the stage where it has a person or group designated as "business development," you need to know how to work with them. This starts by recognizing they are an important member of your team. They are often your company's front line in the marketplace. As such, they are an extremely important source of information about the client, opportunity, and competition.

If your company doesn't have a person or organization identified as BD, someone needs to perform this role for your capture. It may be you or someone else. The following information identifies how the BD role can help you. It walks you through what you'll need to find out and obtain during capture—through whoever is performing the BD role.

Everyone Has A Role

Call plan support

BD should be helpful when you're developing your influence map (see Appendix page 217) and your call plan (see Chapter 15). This includes the customer organization, stakeholders (as appropriate), and competition/potential teaming partners. BD is a great resource to prepare you, your SMEs, and others as your team is executing the call plan. Call plan meetings should be planned—with practice this ensures you have identified in advance what you want to happen as a result of the meeting. The last thing you want is the meeting to have no substantive result and simply end with "I'm glad you came by. It was great talking with you..."

Use a technique such as an empathy map (see Appendix pages 218-220) or other tool to identify the hopes, fears, and biases (project, professional, and personal) of the individual(s) you're going to meet. Use your preparations to maximize your ability to ask insightful questions to stimulate meaningful conversations. Have BD and SMEs help you identify questions to ask to learn details about the project as well as the individual.

If BD or anyone else within your company has an ongoing or past working relationship with the person(s) you're meeting, they should attend at least your first meeting to help your capture team develop a relationship.

Ongoing BD support

BD continues to be an essential member of your team, even after your company makes the decision to pursue an opportunity and appoints you the capture manager. They should be your resource to explain why the opportunity is winnable. This includes identifying the client's motivation for the solicitation and the solution features the client values the most. BD should be able to describe the customer's buying habits, preferences, and specific processes. They need to make you aware of your company's capabilities or offerings as they described them to the client. They also need to describe the client's reactions and any specific areas of interest.

As the capture progresses, you should involve BD in discussions about potential solutions and as a surrogate for the client as you mature your solution. You should include BD in both your formal reviews and proposal reviews to ensure your proposal is compliant, compelling, and convincing.

In addition to working with potential clients, BD also plays an important role in identifying potential teammates, as well as potential competitors. In some cases, BD will present the opportunity to management along with teaming recommendations. These recommendations are often based on their perceptions about the client's relationships with these companies, rather than whether you've considered these companies to be part of your solution. You should ask BD to identify companies already doing business with the client organization, as well as those seeming to be targeting them. Throughout the capture, BD should continue to be your eyes and ears in the marketplace. They need to continue collecting information about companies calling on the client or advertising capabilities that may have a bearing on your capture efforts.

Everyone Has A Role

Chapter 6
The Customer

When we say customer, we are talking about the customer organization—anyone with influence on the procurement you're trying to win. This ranges from those who will influence what is in the RFP to those who may be on the evaluation panel. It is not just the customer Project Manager. It includes all the other influencers and stakeholders, such as the decision authority, acquisition advisors, contracts, and the customer's customers.

"...10 bags of monkey chow, 10 of elephant chow, 10 of ostrich, and 10 of zebra. Please hurry, I felt a drop on the way over."

Playing the Contractor Game to Win

During capture, there are individuals in the customer organization who will be directly or indirectly involved in determining the outcome. You need to figure out who will be influencing the solicitation and the final decision, who will be reviewing and scoring your proposal, who will have the authority to make the source selection, and what authority the contracts and acquisitions staff have. You must also understand how these individuals see the world and what matters to them.

There are times when different departments in the customer's organization will be using the same contract vehicle, and these departments will have differing visions of what they think is important. Knowing the customer also means identifying people who will influence the solicitation and being aware they may not all agree about what the right contractor looks like. Essential to your win strategy is figuring out what success looks like to the various voices impacting the creating of the solicitation and the evaluation of proposals.

Your job is to uncover who has a voice, work to influence their impact on the solicitation, and then develop a solution and a story that will address all those who will be decision-makers.

The influencers

Many people play a role in determining the outcome of a solicitation. This includes people who are not formally involved in writing the solicitation, evaluating the proposals, or briefing the source selection authority. Although they are not directly involved in the acquisition process, these individuals are people to whom those actually doing the work listen.

As capture manager, your job is to identify the potential influencers, understand what message they are delivering, and what effect that message may have on your win strategy. Start by identifying and talking to well-respected authority figures who are not directly involved in the acquisition yet have a relationship with the acquisition. This includes outside advisors and support contractors who are not officially supporting the source selection. You want to figure out the answers to the following questions:

- Are there aspects of the solicitation which reflect the thinking of previous studies/recommendations by outside advisors/support contractors?
- Who are the members of the decision maker's inner circle?
- What is consistent across the potential messages being given to the decision authority and proposal evaluators?
- Are there differing opinions among the influencers in terms of what is important and how to define project success?
- How well does your solution align with those messages?

The stakeholders

Most acquisitions have individuals who are not formal decision makers, yet affect the acquisition, including executives who set requirements, personnel who wield informal power without an official leadership title, or the customer's customer. We refer to these individuals as "stakeholders." These may be people within the buying organization, yet not directly involved in this specific acquisition. Sometimes, the stakeholders may be people outside of the buying organization. This often happens when the opportunity is being acquired by one organization and the ultimate end-user is a different organization. The end-users set requirements, establish success criteria, and make recommendations about potential solutions. Members of the end-user organization may function as formal members of the evaluation team or as advisors.

Below are questions to help obtain information about the stakeholders who are affecting the decision process:

- What organizations will be directly involved in the acquisition?
- What is the buying behavior of the organization leading the acquisition?
- What organization(s) are setting requirements or determining success criteria?
- How do the stakeholders define success?
- What power does the contracts department have?

The evaluators

Often, you'll not be able to identify by name the specific participants in the source selection or their specific roles. Yet you still need to understand who the audience is for your proposal and what process they will follow. This involves identifying what organization is the actual customer and the power structure within their acquisition team. You are trying to understand what will drive the evaluators' decision making.

You want to be able to answer the following questions:

- What level of expertise will the evaluators bring?
- What hopes/fears/biases do the likely evaluators bring? Do they reflect those of their manager or are there divergent hopes/fears/biases represented on the panel?
- Who will likely lead the actual evaluation and/or what are the characteristics of those who have led similar evaluations before?
- How experienced is the contracting officer?
- How do the evaluators define success?
- How well do the likely source selection board members reflect the same perspective as the decision maker(s)?

The decision authority

Even when you can't identify the decision authority by name, you need to identify the level within the organization where the decision will be made. This is the ultimate audience for your proposal and needs to factor into determining your win strategy. Again, you want to be able to answer these questions:

- What is the organizational level where the decision will be made?
- What is the basis for placing the decision at that level (e.g., dollar amount, organizational independence, domain knowledge)?
- Who is likely to be the decision authority?
- What hopes/fears/biases does the likely decision authority bring?
- How involved is the decision authority in shaping the acquisition strategy?
- How likely is it the decision authority will influence the solicitation?
- How likely is it the decision authority will accept the source selection board recommendation without sending them back to re-examine portions of their findings?

Using the answers

The next step is to determine what effect the answers have on your win strategy. The point is to not market or write exclusively to just one segment of your audience. For instance, if you only speak and write to what you think the decision authority wants and miss what the evaluation board is expecting to read, you risk receiving a score you cannot overcome. Or if you don't identify and address the strong bias of one influencer for or against a specific aspect of your solution, that influencer might have a greater effect on the merits of your solution than anything you write.

Make sure you're "talking" to as many of "the right people" as you can identify. And even if you talk to "the right people," be careful not to incorrectly weigh the importance of a particular person's input on the decision:

- You may think the most senior person is the one who will make the decision. However, depending on the work and the organization, writing of the requirements, evaluation, and decision making may happen at a much lower level even for a large project.

- On the other hand, you may think you know who runs the program and who has served on the evaluation panel before, and you assume they will be making this decision. But the decision maker may, in fact, be higher up or lower down in the organization, and you may not know that person's view regarding the project. This makes you susceptible to a competitor coming in and convincing the decision maker a certain aspect of staffing or management or product is essential.

Watch out!!!

Study the customer and their acquisition strategy to identify surprises. These include items pointing to a competitor's fingerprints, items identifying another part of the organization you have not addressed, and things that have been left unsaid (e.g., the government PM sees cutting-edge solutions as high risk). During the capture, pay attention to any new influencers who bring their own biases to the process. Be aware of changes in direction within the client shop that occur before the solicitation drops. And of course, keep your eyes open on your competitors and be aware of personnel they have hired who may have come from your client organization or have a strong relationship with them.

"Try to stay on his good side."

Gatthering What You need

Section 3
Gathering What You Need

"...and it must be true, because we found it on the Internet."

Chapter 7
Collecting Information About—Everything

As capture manager, you're the one responsible for setting expectations in terms of what type of information is needed, how to obtain it, how it is organized, how it is stored, how it is shared across the capture team, how it is used, who needs to know what, and how they find it.

Your starting point is knowing the ground truth: the mission of the project as perceived across the influencers in the customer organization; the current environment—physical, political, technological; and the vision for the future as perceived by the influencers (as discussed earlier, don't assume they all have the same vision). Research is how you lay the foundation—making sure you know enough to have intelligent conversations, ask interesting questions, have the client see you as adding value, and figure out what you need to do to differentiate yourself from everyone else who wants this work. This is true whether you're the incumbent, this is a takeaway from another contractor, or this is new work.

As you work through information collection, you'll see the questions we present are repeated, with a different focus each time, as you move forward in the process. Capture requires this method of asking questions in different ways and at different times to uncover what we don't know.

Gathering What You need

"...oooo and in '82 you forgot to say please!"

Why you collect information

There is a barrage of information coming at you and the members of your capture team. It's coming from conversations, debriefs of conversations, social media, standard media, other research, solution development, discussions based on recruiting, and many other sources. So the basic process requires you to decide what information to collect, manage it as a valuable resource, filter it appropriately to identify what is critical, and provide it to the people who need it. How can you accomplish this most effectively?

Stay curious. Question. Stay focused. Think of yourself as the coach of your capture team. If you were the coach of a sports team, for example, you gather as much information as you can on your players, on the conditions of the field, and on all aspects of the competition. And you would need to weigh all this information to determine what would help you to be best prepared for the game. To the sports coach, there is never too much game film. And for you, there is never too much information. Collecting information is only the first step; you also need to evaluate it and determine what you can use most effectively to be successful.

Your objective is to gather information from various sources—information databases, social media, attending relevant conferences, meetings and seminars, and more. You need to gather and then figure out how to understand the information you gather from your client's perspective. You need to use it to identify what you don't yet know (but need to know) about the customer organization, the opportunity, the requirements, the competitive environment, and how your company is perceived. Remember, your goal is to develop a successful win strategy.

Information you need about the opportunity

With respect to the opportunity, you need to understand:

- Is this a brand-new opportunity or a follow-on contract?
- What is the customer's motivation for conducting the acquisition (is the current contract expiring, have the customer's needs changed)?
- If it's a follow-on or add-on, are they opening it to competition because of procurement rules or because they want to find an alternative source?
- If they are looking for a new source, is it because of price, quality, competency, or something else?
- What is the purpose of the opportunity from the perspective of the direct customer and of influencers within the customer organization (don't assume they're the same)?
- What is the scope of the opportunity—what are they really looking for (e.g., do they want the VW bug, an SUV, a hybrid, or an all-electric vehicle)?
- What is the need behind the need (what are the mission/business imperatives driving the need)?
- Are they open to and/or interested in a new contractor?
- What type of contract is it (e.g., cost-plus, time-and-materials, fixed-price)?

Playing the Contractor Game to Win

Most government opportunities have a long sales cycle—some up to multiple years. During this time, the answers to these questions can change. The acquisition strategy and budget can change. Sometimes the customer organization or personnel can change. Also, the customer is hearing from lots of folks, both inside and outside their organization, and using those inputs to refine their thinking about what they need and how best to solve their problem. Even during shorter cycles, things can change. You must continually revisit what you think you know about the opportunity and make sure it is current.

"Kid, it's never too early to begin your data gathering."

The deal

As you define what the opportunity represents to your company, avoid using the customer's terms and description. Rather, start with a definition of the "the deal." What we mean by the deal is (1) what's in it for your company? and (2) what will it take to win? You need to understand the value of the opportunity to the company. Is it short-term revenue growth, is it penetration of a new market, is it long-term profit growth? What is it? Then, you need to understand what it will take to win. Executive management needs to understand both parts of the deal to decide whether to invest in pursuing the opportunity.

The scope

Remember, the scope of the acquisition determines what is part of the contract and what is not. Unless the client is buying a commodity, which can be specified precisely, there will be elements of ambiguity about the technical and programmatic scope. This opens the possibility for the different offerors to bid different approaches. You need to understand what latitude exists based on how the client defines their problem and whether their budget imposes any constraints, as these aspects will impact the solution and your win strategy. The amount of flexibility in the opportunity will often dictate what you can potentially influence during capture.

Gatthering What You need

The requirements

Among the most important information about the opportunity is its list of requirements. You want to identify these requirements before the RFP comes out. If this is a recompete, you may have the old list, and then you need to figure out what has changed or will change. The more you can help the customer define the way they describe the need in the solicitation, the greater your chance of winning. You should supply this help while the customer is formulating their acquisition strategy and requirements. You need to figure out how to go beyond the specific requirements as stated in the RFP (the need behind the need) in ways the customer will see as providing value to them. Whether this is this a brand-new opportunity, a follow-on, or an add-on contract, we provide you with some questions on the next page to ponder. Even if you own the current work, you need to go through these questions as if you wanted to take it away—it is the way to defeat your competitors.

"What elese do you think the bride and groom want?"

The customer organization(s)

You need to understand who is developing the acquisition strategy, documenting the requirements, writing the scope of work, and participating on the source selection. This is the audience for your capture efforts and eventually for your proposal. A technique, such as an influence map (See Appendix page 217), is useful for identifying the players.

You need information about the organizations involved to determine which one(s) may be driving the decision process. Important questions, (referred to earlier in Chapter 6), include the following:

- Acquisition strategy
    - Who is writing the scope?
    - Will those writing the scope be on the evaluation panel?
    - How involved is the source selection authority?
    - What is the buying behavior of the organization leading the acquisition?
    - How do they define success?
    - How influential is the end-user/manager of the item or service being procured?
- Evaluation team
    - Which organization will likely lead the actual evaluation?
    - What organizations will be directly involved, and which will have a limited role?
    - How experienced is the contracting officer and how much power do they have on the selection?

Knowing who matters

The evaluation team's and decision authority's perceptions are based on their respective hopes, fears, and biases. Knowing what effect each person has on the evaluation is vital, including RFP contributors (and those who influence them); stakeholders, and decision-makers.

This means you not only need to know who these people are, you also need to identify each individual's hopes, fears, and biases as they relate to this opportunity, if you can:

- Do they want everything to stay as it is—are they risk averse?
- Do they want some improvements if the risk is not great?
- Are they trying to make a name for themselves?
- Are they interested in new/improved/innovative solutions, and, if so, how do they define those terms? Are their views shared elsewhere within the organization?

Hopes: what individual customers consider the best-case outcome.

Fears: what they fear as an unfavorable outcome.

Biases: the types of solutions they prefer and the types they dislike.

The customer's tolerance for risk can have a significant effect on the scope of the opportunity. As you learn the risk tolerance of key personnel, together with their level of technical understanding and vision for the future, you can tailor your solution to respond to their hopes, fears, and biases.

Questions to ponder

- What's the customer trying to buy (e.g., are they buying a solution, are they buying staff augmentation, or are they buying a unique expertise)?
  - If they are buying a solution, how detailed will the specifications be?
  - If they are buying labor, what is their perception of the right mix of high-tech engineering/science and lower-tech support?
  - If labor, are they buying a specific staffing level or will they ask each bidder to provide a suggested level of effort?
  - What would they like to accomplish that they aren't able to do now?
- What's driving the acquisition?
  - Are the RFP/RFQ requirements structured around the legacy system/process?
  - Is there a new technology/process being implemented that will still be "new" during the procurement phase (upon solicitation release)?
  - Will the solicitation mirror an existing one? If this is a "recompete" will they alter any of the system, process, or staffing requirements?
  - Is the customer fully confident in how they see the solution (management and tech) or are they open to new or different ideas?
  - If they are open, will they provide latitude in the solicitation?

- What opportunities are there to influence the way the requirements are specified?
    - Can you show them, during capture, you can come in with minimal risk and improve their program (faster/better/cheaper)?
    - What do they like about the way the work is done now (e.g., technical work, management)?
    - Can you offer any innovations of interest to them? If so, you need to get them interested during capture, not through a proposal.
    - How will they weigh/evaluate your design or proposed process?
    - How will they weigh/evaluate your methodology?
    - Will they use the bid to set the contract value, or is it an indefinite delivery/indefinite quantity or stand-by contract with the government setting the ceiling?

Hidden requirements

In our experience, only about 50% of the customer's requirements are actually expressed in the RFP. So merely responding to the RFP does not address all of the requirements important to selecting the winner (e.g., there are often unstated preferences, such as the Army wanting the contractor to have Army experience, not Navy experience, even if precisely the same work or the customer prefers fewer teammates rather than many).

About 20% of the customer's total requirements are associated with the customer's environment. Much of this information is available on the Internet in the form of mission statements, organizational charts, program descriptions, budgetary information, press releases, and Congressional testimony. You need to recognize and address the constraints under which the customer is operating and the resulting "requirements behind the requirements" in the RFP.

Another 20% of the customer's total requirements can only be obtained through direct interactions, both with the customer and third parties very familiar with the customer's needs. *These sessions should not be spent describing your capabilities or trying to convince the customer why your standard offering is appropriate.* You need to focus on *listening* and using the conversation to learn about the customer's technical requirements—contractual, fiscal, and programmatic—as well as regulatory concerns.

Gatthering What You need

The remaining 10% of the customer's total requirements are not readily identified, sometimes even by the customer. Reviewing how the customer has conducted previous source selections and the source selection authority's approach to decision making can provide some insight to these hidden requirements.

And remember—knowing the hidden requirements is essential to understanding how the customer organization perceives what it needs. Nonetheless, once the solicitation drops, you must be responsive and only price what is requested.

The details

Once you think you understand both the requirements and the real problems needing solutions, work on identifying the answers to the following questions, which mirror those we posed earlier in this Chapter (see above). They are aimed at understanding how the customer intends to carry out their procurement:

- Are they buying labor, a service, or an end item?
- If labor, what is the mix of high-tech engineering or lower-tech operations support?
- Are they buying a specific staffing level or letting you bid the level of effort you think will be required?
- If a service, how do they intend to determine whether the service was acceptable and what is their view of the required labor mix?
- If an end item, how detailed are the specifications?
- How much are they weighing/evaluating your design?
- How much are they weighing your methodology?
- What type of contract is it (e.g., cost-plus, time-and-materials, fixed-price)?
- Will they use your bid to set the contract value, or is it an indefinite delivery/indefinite quantity contract, with the government setting the ceiling?
- Are they competing it because of procurement rules or because they want to find an alternative source?
- If they are looking for a new source, is it because of price, quality, competency, or something else?
- What latitude is there to propose a different way of meeting the requirements?

Your team

While you're gathering information about the opportunity and the competition, you also need to begin collecting information about your teammates. This is essential to integrating them into the solution and ensuring your team meets all the solicitation requirements. Most often, you use a series of data calls to obtain the information you need. Plan these data calls to avoid overloading the teammates and losing track of the information they provide. If they don't meet your deadline or don't provided the information you requested, follow up quickly to get them accustomed to meeting your deadline.

The initial data call to your teammates should request the following information:

- who they know at the client organization and how they know them;
- what work they have done or are doing within the client organization and provide project descriptions; and
- if they have staff who have worked for or in the client organization, provide their resumes.

The competition

At the same time you're gathering information about the client organization and the opportunity, you also need to be gathering information about your competition and the competitive environment, developing a personality assessment to help you do a better competitive analysis. You want to know/gather:

- How competitive is the opportunity?
  - How many companies are demonstrating an interest in the opportunity?
  - What specific actions is the customer taking to make the procurement competitive (e.g., sources sought, industry days, one-on-one visits, draft solicitation)?
- Who are the competitors—what is their personality profile?
  - Who are the competitors (and remember, you should find ways to talk to them about where they are and why they think they can win)?
  - What relationships do they have and how much access do they have within the client organization?
  - Who are they hiring/trying to hire?
  - How are they perceived within the client organization?
  - Is this a must win for them and how does it fit into their strategy?
  - What is significant to them corporately—what aspects of the acquisition strategy and solution are they pushing?

- Have they made any recent acquisitions?
- Who will likely be their PM and key personnel and how well are they known and liked?
- What solution will they propose?
- Are there any recent successes they will tout?
- How will they price their solution?
- What strengths and weaknesses* do they have?
* How competitive is your team?
  - What can the competition find out about your company, your team, your relationships that matter?
  - What strengths and weaknesses does your company/team have and what differentiates your offer?

Talk to your competition. Call and ask if they are teaming and/or want to talk—it never hurts to talk as long as you minimize what you share to what they could find out elsewhere with a little research. Be prepared to ask open-ended questions.

* Remember, when we refer to strengths and weaknesses, we are talking about how the client will perceive them—both those who have input into developing the solicitation and those who will evaluate the proposals. What your team alone thinks will not help you win.

How to obtain the necessary information

Information on your competition as well as your customer is available through direct customer contacts, contacts with other influencers, and research using various sources, including social media. As you will notice, some of what we recommend applies only to competitors, some only to customers, and some to both.

Direct and Indirect Customer Contact
Customer interactions to develop relationships at various levels within the customer organization are the best way to gather insights about their perspectives. You use this information to shape your solution and develop your win strategy. Since customers often place constraints on the timing and number of interactions, every interaction need not be a formal meeting—find out where they will be, online or in person, and be there. As you gather information and begin to create a perception of the customer from individual influencers, make sure to identify independent sources who can verify your hypothesis. You can also use business interactions and discussions with those who have relationships with the evaluators, people who will influence the evaluators, and where possible, the evaluators themselves.

Whether at their office or at an external event, when you know you'll have the opportunity to have a conversation, come prepared with questions to get the client to talk. The more you know about them, the easier this is. The goal is to get them to articulate their views: what they are satisfied with, their vision for the future, their frustrations, their constraints, and what they are hoping for over the next few years. Remember this is not an interview. You want to engage them in a dialogue.

Preparing open-ended questions is a good way to get them to open up. This requires you to do your homework, understand the client's needs, and bring value. Use your research to ensure you're asking questions and talking about things they care about. And you need to *listen* to their answers without your own biases, conscious or otherwise, getting in the way. Study up on confirmation and other types of bias that can get in your way—we all have these biases and only if we are aware of them can we keep them at bay.

You also need to *listen* for and learn about the customer's technical requirements, contractual and fiscal requirements, and programmatic as well as any regulatory concerns and/or office politics. You need to turn off your filters and personal preferences so you will hear how the client perceives the problem and current biases they have regarding different possible solutions. Their perceptions may be your best guide for developing an offer that meets the customer's needs.

Other sources

Social media is often a good way to gather background information in preparation for a formal meeting and to identify other forums in which casual interaction may be possible. These can include meetings or conferences. Social media may also identify first- and second-level acquaintances who can provide information about the customer's hopes, fears, and biases. As you gather information and begin to create a perception of the customer, make sure to identify independent sources who can verify your hypothesis.

Many medium to large companies have a group who gathers market intelligence. For smaller companies, this becomes the responsibility of the capture team. Agency websites provide good background information on their mission and broad objectives. These sites sometimes include organizational information and the results of past source selections. They may also identify current contracts and the companies performing the work. Another excellent source of information is Freedom of Information Act (FOIA) requests, and these are discussed below.

Here are some ways to obtain information:
- make Freedom of Information Act (FOIA) requests for proposals, contracts, contract modifications, and task orders. Several market research companies make such FOIA requests and provide the results for a fee. Obtaining the information this way can be both more expedient and obscure your company's interest in an opportunity;
- search state-level contracts when your competition is engaged. These "sunshine states" have past proposals available for the asking or on the web;

- review source selection memoranda;
- research websites and Google searches/use Google alerts for recent/relevant press releases;
- review leadership bios (any changes);
- read information on public companies: quarterly and annual reports, earnings calls (what things are getting better, what are they bragging about, what concerns are they addressing); and
- find out if anyone in your organization has worked for the competition or the client—they can be helpful in defining the customer's perception of the competition.

Individual company websites can also provide a wealth of information about the company's offerings, how they describe themselves, and the markets they are targeting. Pay particular attention to presentations made to outside advisors or research groups, as well as their presentations at conferences, their webinar offerings, and the like.

Developing and maintaining relationships with your competitors, who may at times be your team members, makes this part of capture easier. Sure, there is a lot of information on the web, in social media, in published reports, and in presentations. Unfortunately, this information doesn't help you understand enough about what they will do for this particular opportunity and/or how they will come at it. People who work for your competitors belong to many of the same professional organizations as you, and throughout your career, as you work for different companies and/or hire individuals from various companies, you can grow your network and develop sources of information. You should get to the point where you can pick up the phone and have a conversation with a contact at another company about an opportunity.

How to organize your information

Start with Storage! As you begin to gather information about the customer, the opportunity, and the competition have a definite plan about how and where to store this information. Today, nearly every company from start-ups to Fortune 100s has some type of information repository accessible through the web. The problem is these repositories quickly become dumping grounds where information goes to die. Figuring out where to store your information, think first about the basics: how do you intend to collect, organize, and file the results of customer meetings, information gathered from FOIA requests, and information gathered through web searches? Even with decent search capabilities and a logical folder structure, it may be too difficult to find relevant information quickly and efficiently. As more and more information is added to the files, identifying potentially valuable information becomes increasingly difficult. You cannot simply direct your proposal team to a repository with hundreds or thousands of separate documents (including miscellaneous documents such as contact reports, step reviews, customer presentations and competitive analyses) and expect them to find the salient information from an ad hoc search. You need to provide yourself and your team with the proper tools to find what you are looking for.

Gathering What You need

Best practices to help you manage your capture data

- Every week, review what is new, making sure you have identified important new data and have ensured its connection to the right individuals and the right space within your capture plan.
- Use collaborative software to "chat" with the entire team on something posted or you can select just one or more individuals for specific conversations. The beauty of this process versus email is it places everything about the opportunity, including these conversations, in one location, in searchable form.
- Add new data in a way that notifies your team members it is there. Have your team set themselves up to be notified once a day when new information is added or there are any changes to data.
- Set up an organizational structure to separate different parts of the capture information to make it easier to find things—client information and relationships, competitive information and relationships, teaming (including NDAs (Non-Disclosure Agreements), TAs (Teaming Agreements), relevant information, solutions, staffing, past solicitations/proposals, price/PTW (keep this one locked to just those who need access), and the like.
- Within each folder, set up an archive folder for what might be outdated information.
- Use the features of your collaborative tools to maintain a log of everything being placed into storage, the date it was put in, who put it in, and a few words about why it matters.

Analyze and categorize

Find time each day to review everything coming in and don't prejudge the value or meaning of any information. **Remember, assumptions cut off data flow.** As you develop your own emotional intelligence, you become more aware of your own biases and how they can affect your reactions to what you read, listen to, or watch (to learn more about emotional intelligence, see bibliography for selected readings on the topic). The goal is to be open so you don't miss, misinterpret, or misunderstand information or data. Listen for any underlying concerns being expressed. This is imperative to working your win strategy successfully.

Be skeptical about information until you have validated it and keep validating information as the capture evolves. Remember one data point is simply an anecdote; it takes multiple data points over time (including from BD) to develop defensible data. Taking information at face value and without appropriate validation can put you on the wrong path.

As noted above, you need to start collecting and storing information very early in your capture effort. It's amazing how quickly information can pile up; it can become overwhelming and nearly useless if you can't find what you need easily and efficiently. Use an organizational structure that is simple and makes it easy to find and use by your team—set up clear, concise categories such as client info, competition info, solution/issue analysis, pricing, and staffing.

Chapter 8
Key Personnel and Staffing

If you're just providing a widget with no support, key personnel and staffing may not play much of a role. However, when you're providing support or providing a service, what matters most is who is managing the effort and with whom the customer will be working. Customers care deeply about the people they will end up working with on the contract.

If the work is currently being done by another company, what does their staffing look like and at what price? If you're the incumbent, you need to take a hard look not only at how you're doing this now, but also at how you're staffed and whether your staff have become too senior or too expensive for what needs to be done. If your competition can come in cheaper with qualified people, you can easily lose on price. On the other hand, if the opportunity is for new work, you should explore how the client likes things managed and staffed on comparable programs. Whatever the situation, you need to make sure your key personnel and staff match up well with the opportunity and the customer in terms of both qualifications and cost.

Playing the Contractor Game to Win

"Okay, what other qualifications do you have?"

Key personnel

When thinking about key personnel, here are questions to ask and answer honestly:
- Is each key individual known, and, if so, respected within the client organization?
- If any of your key personnel aren't known by the client organization, how do you make them known or make sure their resumes resonate with the evaluators?
- Is a highly qualified (or possibly overqualified) technical person the right choice?
- If the individuals are known within the industry, is there any negative press or other information about them you may have to address?
- Are the key personnel at the right price points for this client organization?
- When thinking about the program manager, the management team, and SMEs, what do you know about previous successful projects with this customer?
- Has the customer indicated a preference for working with individuals with particular skill sets...even hinted at specific people?
- Has the customer expressed preferences about what the project teams should look like?

Staffing

Staffing is an important part of your solution. It is usually the major component of your cost and a significant driver in how you price your proposal. As capture manager, you need to start with your win strategy: your staffing approach needs to reflect your win strategy and enable you to deliver the solution you're proposing. As you gather information about the opportunity and develop your staffing approach, you need to answer these questions:

- Is staffing only being evaluated as part of your price or is it also being evaluated as part of your management or technical approach?
  - Does the client's cost evaluation model prescribe the staffing level or is it up to you to propose one?
  - Will the client downgrade your technical or management score if you propose the wrong staffing level?
- What knowledge, skills, and abilities are driven by your solution?
- What knowledge, skills, and abilities are important to the customer?
- Does the customer have a specific idea about the staffing required or are they open to alternative approaches?

- If this is a follow-on contract:
  - Is the customer concerned about retention of the incumbent workforce?
  - Do they want to retain part or all of the current workforce?
  - How open are they to, or interested in, introducing new skills/talents?
  - Does your solution provide ways to make the workforce more efficient or eliminate staff with inflated salaries?
- Is there a difference between the day-one staffing level and other times during the contract (e.g., changes due to life cycle phases, implementation of automation)? If there are variations over time, what is the basis for these variations and how does your staffing approach ensure the changes are handled efficiently?

You should be sure to vet your staffing ideas within the client organization wherever and whenever possible.

Letting the customer see who they are hiring (when possible)

Make the time for your proposed key individuals to interface with the client organization—the more touches the better, both in person (offices, meetings, conferences, industry gatherings) and, based on the organization, through social media. This includes people who may not technically be considered "key personnel," yet may be important to your solution or filling other roles that may be important to the customer. If you have key and/or important personnel from your subcontractors, make sure to include them in these interfaces to show you're one team. And you need to determine if you can win using strong contingent hires as opposed to current employees, even if this precludes introducing them to the customer prior to your proposal. Remember many evaluators are not the higher management staff, so make these connections and touches throughout the organization to maximize your win potential.

Working with human resources

Your human resources personnel can be invaluable to the capture effort. You need their support in determining how best to recruit the required staff and in developing the Compensation Plan. The Compensation Plan includes at least the following decisions:

- whether to provide a tailored benefits package for the new hires;
- how best to approach any incumbent staff;
- whether to conduct early recruiting activities (e.g., targeted advertisements, online searches, open houses);
- which personnel you might hire early and which will be contingent hires; and
- the steps to take for a realistic phase-in.

Your recruiter's role

Your job is to make sure your recruiters help you win by doing more than just finding the right staff. They also should be gathering information to help you develop the right solution and better define the PTW. What they can learn through online resources and through staffing firms (some of which your company may have on contract) will help drive your capture strategy.

Whether the opportunity is a new one or a recompete, there are usually people who are already performing at least some of the requested services for the customer. They may be on the current project or a different project. These may be people the customer wants you to include in your staffing solution. These current and former contractor staff will have knowledge of the opportunity. Your recruiters are best equipped to find them, contact them, learn competitive information, and as needed, get them committed to your team. And the earlier you bring in your recruiters, the easier it will be for them to get you what you need to position your team to win. They are a part of your capture team—they should participate in capture meetings, as appropriate, depending on the size and nature of recruiting activities.

In summary, don't be bashful about asking your recruiter to put on their BD hat. They should be looking for information about the incumbent, competitors, and personnel currently performing the same or similar work. They may find you information about current salaries, subject matter experts (SMEs) who have answers only an incumbent will know, or former incumbents/customer employees who can serve both as contributors to the proposal and as key personnel.

How you can help your recruiter

You can help your recruiters by identifying organizations, associations, educational institutions, and unique places to identify candidates. Also, working with your technical staff, it is your job to provide your recruiters with requisitions that identify the experience you need, and to develop lines of questions you know will help them weed out unqualified candidates.

You should also determine whether a senior recruiter or even the manager from human resources is needed to bring value and/or take value from participating in your capture meetings.

Playing the Contractor Game to Win

CHAPTER 9
PICKING THE RIGHT TEAMMATES

Gatthering What You need

One of the hardest capture jobs—especially when you're the prime—is identifying and securing companies that would make good teammates. You'll receive lots of advice about which companies to add to the team, not all of which is consistent. You'll likely be approached by companies seeking a role on your team or looking to have you on their team. The preferences of members of your capture team might not be aligned with corporate guidelines or your win strategy.

Gap analysis will help you make the right choices. Based on what you know about the customer and their perceptions of what is needed for success, you need to conduct a thorough gap analysis considering:

- your customer's preferences (are certain companies always on the winning team?);
- your company's real and perceived weaknesses a teammate can remedy (be specific); and
- socioeconomic requirements.

The internal politics

Building your team requires you to navigate issues and weigh trade-offs. You need to determine what your A team will look like—what each member should bring to the team (e.g., relationships, technical expertise, capacity, small business status), at what price. You also need to have some ideas for alternatives, as you can't always get exactly what you want.

Your management may push you to include a teaming partner they are trying to team with elsewhere or have a "quid pro quo" coming due. Similarly, one of your SMEs may have a favorite team member to whom they owe a favor. Management may also be focused on the work share they must give up or other commitments this teaming arrangement may allow them to meet. Such choices may favor companies who are less than optimal for your opportunity.

Your job is to remain loyal to your win strategy. As capture manager, you need to know how teaming fits your win strategy. This allows you to convince your team, your management, and a potential teaming partner why teaming represents the right approach for this opportunity. A bad teaming decision can jeopardize the capture in many ways, such as pricing, compliance, and meeting their responsibilities for timely and succinct inputs.

And remember, don't team with someone and give them work share just to take them off the street unless you're sure they can beat you!

Teammate criteria

How do you decide, and then convince those involved, this team is the winning team? You start by identifying companies meeting these criteria:

- they help you to tell the evaluation team a story they find credible and compelling;
- they fill a clearly defined role essential to winning (i.e., they offer a required capability your team does not currently have);
- they represent a good choice to provide the capability/ socioeconomic status;
- they both fill the capability gap *and* are available at a price consistent with achieving your PTW;
- their work share commitment is commensurate with the incremental improvement they bring to your win possibility;
- they are able and willing to commit the necessary level of capture and proposal support;
- they allow your company to manage to profit objectives; and
- they are not viewed negatively by evaluators in the client organization.

Chapter 10
Other Skills You May Need

"Very impressive, but those are not the kind of web skills we're looking for."

Gatthering What You need

Increase your impact by finding the people who can help you:

- provide webinars for relevant associations/organizations;
- make presentations at meetings, seminars, workshops;
- prepare printed materials addressing the client's needs;
- write blogs and/or editorials, and white papers; and
- add pages and/or updating information on your company's website.

These materials and activities greatly enhance your capture efforts. To improve their quality and effectiveness, you need to have access to a wide range of skills and talents, including the following:

Marketing folks—*graphic artists, presentation experts*— are individuals who have a great sense of visual presentation. They know how to create strong graphics, choose the right photos and illustrations, and present information in ways that resonate with the client. Pithy presentation of data lets people take in information in ways that connect with them and hold their attention.

Web authors are experts who can help you tailor your website by making it more informative and attractive, identifying weak points and areas for improvement, and collecting information on how people view your materials online.

Blog writers are individuals who know how to grab interest, write clearly and succinctly, and are not focused on selling. They can help you share important information with readers you are trying to reach. These pieces can be posted to social media, sent to email lists you have, placed on your website, etc.

Technical experts and editors are experts who can develop white papers to create interest in what you're doing or thinking.

You can't do it all yourself. Without these individuals, you limit your ability to communicate with your client—and with potential clients. The content you produce with the help of these experts can also help you to attract potential team members—including talented individuals and other companies.

Gatthering What You need

CHAPTER 11
CAPTURE MANAGEMENT CONSULTANTS

"Hang on, the consultant just flew in."

A lot of companies use consultants to help win new business. Consultants help BD gain access to customers or provide additional insights about a specific opportunity. Many times, consultants are used to fill important proposal roles, from proposal manager to volume manager to SME to price-to-win.

In today's hyper-competitive government services market, firms often benefit from the support of a senior capture management consultant. A senior capture management consultant is an independent expert who has selected capture management as a career, is a student of the profession, and has repeatedly demonstrated the ability to win. If you don't have someone on your in-house staff to fill this role for a critical capture, a senior capture management consulting arrangement is a cost-effective way for the company to gain an expert, a mentor, an extra pair of hands, and a collaborator.

Consultant as capture expert

When you hire an outside capture manager to run a pursuit, this demonstrates to your staff this is an important opportunity and provides concrete evidence of your willingness to invest in growth. This capture manager is responsible for developing the capture strategy and then making sure the capture team executes the strategy. The capture manager will make decisions on how to proceed based on their judgment. The consultant is expected to be responsive and provide the assistance required—they are expected to be involved in the technical details or monitor their work daily. The capture manager consultant should work out the expectations about communications and how progress will be reported. The consultant's role is to solve the immediate problem—position your company to win a specific opportunity.

Consultant as mentor

Your consultant can mentor your capture team led by someone else. Here, the consultant's responsibilities are different from managing the capture. The consultant is still considered the *expert*; the consultant just isn't responsible for running the pursuit, the capture manager is. The consultant serves as an advisor, monitoring and assessing the work of the team. They lead workshops, review documentation, facilitate strategy sessions, and provide the benefit of their years of experience.

Using the consultant in this manner is often less expensive than having them manage the capture. Yet it demonstrates your commitment to pursuing the opportunity and exposes your staff to what a senior capture manager actually can do to position a company for a win.

Consultant as "extra pair of hands"

Another way to use a senior capture management consultant is to augment your current capture resources. This may include direct support to you as the assigned capture manager, and participation on review and recovery teams. In any one of these cases, as capture manager, you retain full control, and the consultant applies their specialized knowledge to specific parts of the process to "get it done." The consultant is expected to implement action plans to achieve the vision you have developed.

The capture management consultant is also expected to make suggestions for your review. The consultant's goal is to make the capture effort as efficient and effective as they can while working to support you as the capture manager.

Consultant as collaborator

When you elect to use the capture management consultant as a collaborator, problem-solving becomes a joint venture. The senior capture management consultant is bringing their specialized knowledge of capture and combining it with your knowledge of the organization to help you solve a problem. The problem may be how to create a more growth-oriented culture, expand the company's addressable market, or win more jobs with better profitability.

A senior capture management consultant brings a broad perspective on how to effectively research, identify, analyze, and bring new services to market. These skills have been honed over many years and can help your company to launch enduring and productive market expansion strategies. While many entrepreneurs in small and mid-sized companies have the necessary skills, collaborating with a senior capture management consultant introduces new competencies and a different perspective.

Gathering What You need

CHAPTER 12
ADAPTING TO THE SITUATION

Throughout this book we talk about the importance of being curious and getting to the need behind the need. The more tools you have, the more effective you'll be as a capture manager. As capture manager, you need to engage your team and your client, whether in two or three dimensions.

Bottom line—continually look for new methods to help your team perform better, based on their strengths and weaknesses.

"Here's a nickel—spend it wisely!"

Virtual collaboration

As we write this book, we are getting back from COVID-19, which had most of us working with our clients using various audio and visual communication technologies. As we go to whatever the new normal is, remote interaction will continue to be a greater part of the business world. You can operate virtually and still facilitate full engagement if you take the time to learn how. Get comfortable using available tools (which will continually change).

Engaging with your team

- Learn to look into that little dot on your computer that is your camera—it is how you look someone in the eye.
- Learn to use Whiteboard and to share documents and enable everyone on the call to participate.
- Learn to use polls and other tools to engage everyone.
- Use stickies on your desk for each person on the call so you don't leave any voices out of the conversation—the visual reminder can often make a difference.
- Learn to draw in Word, on PowerPoint or using any other tool (or have someone who can do that on the call) as a "people solution"—just as if you were in the same room.
- Take notes (or have someone else take them) so everyone can see—and comment. It keeps people engaged (most of us cannot afford visual facilitation experts for our everyday meetings).

Engaging with your client

- Remember that dot on your computer that is your camera.
- Share photos they might like or find humorous—you need to know what will be acceptable, but this is one way to be human.
- Based on their level of comfort, share a whiteboard or other tool so you can all make notes, comment, etc., as appropriate.
- If presenting, make sure to pause and ask questions as you have no body language to use for cues.
- Decide when to turn on camera shots of participants to provide facial cues—and pay attention to those cues.
- Do NOT look at your phone or do something else during a meeting—anyone watching people's faces can easily tell who is listening, who is not.

Resources and tools for capture are continually evolving. The reading list at the end of this book includes articles on everything from facilitation to managing a team, managing by influence, effective presentations, effective writing, and emotional intelligence.

Facilitation

Techniques to help you to facilitate meetings are particularly important for capture management. Most of us need training and reminders in this area. You'll be facilitating one-on-one meetings; facilitating large and small groups, virtually and in person; facilitating to get at different types of information—relationships, connections, solutioning, and more. Much depends on your ability to find ways to engage your team and ensure everyone has a voice. They need to be able to share information about the client and the client's world, influencers, processes and tools that may be part of the solution, and more.

There are lots of books and tools for facilitation. They provide methods for getting at information. You can check the two resources referenced below, while you take the time to research on your own, as the tools and processes continue to change.

The Grove (https://www.thegrove.com/) provides training and tools for visual and virtual facilitation to improve your virtual and in-person facilitation skills. It includes methods and techniques for you to use to make sure everyone's voice is heard and to enable you to run great, effective meetings with agendas, goals, and focus.

There is also a wide range of books out there that address facilitation. We have had great results with a book called "Gamestorming":

Gamestorming: A Playbook for Innovators, Rulebreakers, and Changemakers is a great playbook to help you get the most out your capture team. Developed for marketers, there is nothing magical here, but it is a compilation of fun facilitation techniques to get your team out of your "we're great" space and into what the barriers to winning might be, ways to identify who you need to know and talk to, ways to identify and think about what is driving your client and their organization, and more. An important part of the Gamestorming approach to facilitation is giving time and space for individuals to think on their own before sharing—as both individual and group-think are important if you want to maximize the potential of your capture team. (Also check out their website: gamestorming.com.)

Section 4
How to Inspire the Client to Choose You

"Together we're irresistable!

CHAPTER 13
VALUE PROPOSITION

Your "value proposition" is what the *customer perceives* as the benefit of selecting your offering. Though not sufficient by itself, it is necessary to make your proposal a winner. A compelling value proposition needs to meet the following three criteria:

1. Specific: it explains how you will improve their situation.
2. Need-focused: it explains how you will address the customer's real requirements.
3. Exclusive: it explains why the customer can only get the perceived value by selecting you and not the competition.

The customer doesn't have a reason to work with you over someone else unless they see the unique value you bring. Your value proposition can't be a slogan, catch phrase, or a bunch of buzz words strung together. It needs to be written in the language of the customer. It describes your solution and the benefit of that specific solution. You should determine your value proposition at the beginning of your capture and then continue to evolve it throughout the capture effort. The final validation of your value proposition occurs during the debrief after you've won.

Evaluate your value proposition by checking whether it answers these questions:

- What specifically are you selling?
- How does this meet the customer's requirements?
- What makes your offering unique?

The best value proposition is clear. What it is. Why it's beneficial. And who benefits. It needs to be easy to understand. It needs to communicate the concrete results the customer will get from selecting your company.

Finding what makes your offering unique is often hard. It requires deep self-reflection and an understanding of what the customer values—what they really care about. There's no point in being unique for the sake of being unique. You don't have to be unique to the whole world, just in the customer's mind.

How To Inspire The Client

Three examples of value propositions that won work.

1. Our solution leverages specific expertise available from our staff to assess the impact of regulatory changes and ensure continued regulatory compliance. The proposed staff are already working with a client to provide this service. Leading our team is a nationally renowned policy expert who is not just a name—she will be engaged through project completion, participating in the kick-off and every monthly meeting. The project team brings the expertise, relevant hands-on successes, and needed relationships with the regulatory agencies to get the work done right, meeting all regulatory compliance and schedule requirements while providing the technical expertise needed for on-time project completion.

2. Our solution integrates automation into the claims processing workflow. This increases speed, accuracy, and consistency, which translates into time and cost savings. Our approach meets the claims processing requirement with very limited manual intervention. Our recent experience automating the claims workflow resulted in a 20% increase in productivity with the same number of people allowing our client to significantly reduce their claims processing backlog.

3. Our solution incorporates use of an assessment software tool to find candidates who have behavioral and technical traits well suited for the customer's highly demanding environment. By using this tool in conjunction with the conventional interview process we can make better hiring decisions, reduce employee turnover, and create better employee development programs. This assessment tool is currently being used on Program XYZ and has resulted in 99% of staff successfully completing the very demanding training and certification requirements.

Chapter 14
What's the Difference between a Win Strategy and a Win Theme

Win Strategy vs. Win Theme

Capture teams often confuse "win strategy" and "win theme." While related, they are two distinct aspects to a winning effort.

The win *strategy* is your plan for HOW to win the opportunity. It identifies what you need to do to win (e.g., relationship building/maintenance, staffing, teaming, solutioning, pricing). It needs to be worked and evolved based on information you obtain and actions you take during the capture process. Your formal reviews (see Chapter 3) require you to articulate your current win strategy and explain how it gets you to the win. This leads to more focused capture efforts and better-informed bid/no-bid decisions.

By contrast, win *themes* are how to convince the customer WHY they want you. Based on information gathered, you'll identify how to best articulate the value you bring to this client in a way that speaks directly to your client's needs and biases.

"I hope you have data to back up all that iambic pentameter."

How To Inspire The Client

Determine your win strategy

Your win strategy is driven by information about the opportunity, the client, your competition, and your company. It requires careful analysis of where you are in the eyes of the influencers and evaluators. It should tell you what you need to do to get to the point where they want to work with your team. Your win strategy is developed by the capture team and managed by you, the capture manager.

The win strategy guides your actions to get to the win. It is not written in the proposal or briefed to the client. The initial win strategy should be developed as part of the initial pursuit decision. It evolves as you learn more/do more about the deal, the client, the stakeholders, the competition, and your team. If it doesn't evolve, something is not working right. For example, when the capture starts, an important piece of your win strategy may be to find a way to discuss the project with a certain part of the customer organization. The part of the organization you know will be involved in writing the SOW (Statement of Work) and will have one or two people on the evaluation panel. Once you do that and begin developing that relationship, your win strategy changes. Based on those discussions you may find out about one of their favorite contractors. So, guess what? Getting that company or, minimally, some of the folks from that company who they love, on your team could become a key to your win strategy.

Part of your job is to continually identify and revise your strategy, what you need to do to win. Approach does not drive your strategy, strategy drives your approach. At all times, your strategy needs to be understood by the capture team, acceptable to your company management, and executable.

Examples of win strategies

The following are examples of win strategies. You might choose one strategy or a combination of different strategies, depending on the specifics of the opportunity and who you are as a company:

1. Convince the influencers to require a certain expertise or level of experience to ensure their project's success (if you know it eliminates significant competitors).
2. Convince them to loosen the experience requirements to enable greater competition from companies like yours.
3. Convince the acquisition team to make the bid multiple award so you can win a slot (if you know you can't displace the incumbent).
4. Convince the acquisition team to make it single award (if you believe you can win it all).
5. Hire the PM and/or subject matter experts you know the client trusts and wants as their contractor's manager.
6. Convince them of the risk of going with another provider (problems they have had, issues, lack of certain expertise).
7. Find a way to develop the best relationships with the influencers and decision-makers.
8. Have the lowest price.
9. Convince the influencers and evaluators the quality and innovation you offer is what they need and should be highly weighted in the evaluation criteria.

How To Inspire The Client

"Are you sure there's nothing in the rules against jet-assist?"

Work your strategy

If your win strategy is to be the lowest price, you need to understand how to reach that price. If your strategy is to offer an innovative solution that provides higher quality and/or better results, you must have the relationships to understand what the customer will consider innovative and what they will be willing to pay. Then, once you develop your solution, vet those ideas within the customer organization. Sometimes a strategy will require working with the customer's contract shop (e.g., making it multiple-award, taking out or putting in certain requirements). Sometimes it will require giving them ideas of what to include in the solicitation to ensure their success. And sometimes it will be about hiring people you don't yet have or teaming with specific companies. Remember, test your strategy throughout the capture within the client organization, in formal reviews, in meetings with your management, with your SMEs, and within the capture team.

Your win themes— the BENEFIT you bring

Purpose

The purpose of win themes is to help the customer understand why your offer is the best for them from their perspective. A strong win theme answers the question: WHAT IS IN IT FOR ME TO PICK YOU?

The specific wording of themes often evolves during capture and then again while writing the proposal. However, when you start the proposal process, you need to take what you developed during capture and ensure all authors know what the themes are and why they are important to the win.

A win theme is neither an assertion nor a superficial promise. It must clearly reflect what you learned your client cares about and be substantiated by aspects of your approach. If you have done a good job during capture, the benefits (your win themes) will clearly tie to the client's decision criteria in the solicitation and can be rated as a strength. During capture you need to validate what you have determined matters most to those who write the solicitation and to those who will evaluate the proposals. And remember, wording and tone matter. They are part of what you learn during capture. You want to know what tone will connect and what vocabulary they use to describe what success looks like.

Remember your themes MUST be consistent with your final win strategy. If your final win strategy is to offer the lowest price, then your win themes should provide your customer with confidence you can meet their requirements at the lowest price. If your final win strategy focuses instead on an innovative or technically superior product, your win themes must still emphasize the benefits your client will experience—the benefits you know they care about.

Validation

Win themes are like a tree—the roots and trunk are your main value proposition—the benefits perceived by the customer. Use each branch (each section) to validate your win themes by substantiating the benefits of your solution including your technical solution, your staffing and management solutions, your experience, past performance, and, finally, pricing.

For example, if you have learned the client's primary concern is meeting the schedule and price is of a lesser concern, then an overall win theme should be about your ability to guarantee on-time delivery. During capture, as you dialogue within the client organization, find out why adhering to schedule matters to them—what is behind this need to meet schedules and their concerns regarding any misses.

In selecting your Program Manager, you need to make sure she has experience meeting all schedule requirements in previous engagements. Your technical approach needs to show a focus of on-time delivery. Your staffing needs to validate you have sufficient staff to meet schedule requirements. Your experience and/or past performance needs to validate you have conducted similar work and met and/or exceeded schedules. And your pricing supports meeting all schedule constraints. During capture, as you pull the pieces together, the win theme needs to guide your decision-making.

Evolution

The win themes evolve throughout the capture, as you learn more about what the client really cares about. During capture, when in conversation with individuals within the customer organization, you should gauge their responsiveness to your win themes—do they articulate what the client experiences as important and necessary for the program? When done correctly, this is one way the proposal continues your conversation with the client. Proposals must reflect the win strategy. Be tied to the client's decision criteria. And be reinforced by the contents of the proposal. If you have strong win themes, you'll hear them repeated back to you during the debrief of the win.

Tying Your Win Themes Together – You Try It

During capture, you determine your win themes through your research, your conversations, and your analysis. As part of this analysis, you need to tie your win themes together into a cohesive story that will resonate with the evaluators, remembering not all evaluators will necessarily define success in the same way. The complexity will be determined by the opportunity and the client organization—how many different pieces of the organization do you need to "speak" to in your proposal, your final conversation.

When you get to pre-proposal and the proposal stage, before you assign the writers their pieces of the outline, explain how the win theme applies to each piece of the proposal. Then make sure those themes are clear and supported.

Chapter 15
Developing and Executing Your Call Plan

You need an opportunity-specific call plan whether you're the incumbent trying to keep the work, a competitor trying to beat the incumbent, or pursuing a totally new opportunity. The call plan is your way of tracking who at the customer or competition organization should be contacted, who should make the contact, why you're making the contact, what you learned, and what are your next steps.

Usually, some amount of work has gone into identifying and qualifying the opportunity. Hopefully, this included customer calls and relationship building. Though fine for qualifying the opportunity, they aren't adequate to win. You need information which can only be obtained through continuing interactions with the people involved in determining the requirements, creating the solicitation, evaluating the proposals, and making the decision. Whether you make the calls yourself or not, these interactions need to be planned, coordinated, and tracked.

How To Inspire The Client

"If you are calling to schedule a meeting, press 1. If you are trying to schedule a meeting with senior staff, press 2 and call back five more times. If you are calling to schedule a meeting with senior management, press 3, followed by the # sign and 500 words on why we won't be wasting our time when we could be eating lunch."

Developing your call plan

You can use a spreadsheet, text table, database, or customer relationship management (CRM) system, such as Dynamics or Salesforce. The point is to have something easy to populate and update; accessible by multiple people. The call plan does not need to contain a lot of detail. That detail belongs in the contact reports.

Next, to be able to manage the call plan and hold your team to account, you need to develop a matrix, similar to the one below, to keep on a shared platform. As discussed in Chapter 5, you can help your SMEs become more comfortable with this process, reminding them they are talking to individuals who care about the same things they care about, and the goal is to do great work for them.

An effective call plan identifies what your objective is for each meeting. It could be a follow-on meeting, an introduction to an influencer, or an invitation to provide a demonstration. You get the idea—you don't want the conversation to end without a next step. The combination of the call plan and contact report are essential to ensure the capture team does not miss someone, is consistent with the information they share, and is neither redundant nor contradictory.

Name/title / Acquisition Role*	Contact Info	Likes/ dislikes/ biases**	Who	Supporting information & materials needed	Date Due	Completed

*Acquisition role: Influencers, procurement author, evaluator, decision authority, contracts

**Likes/dislikes/biases: Should include how they currently feel about your company (love, like, don't care, have an issue)

Maintaining your call plan

Initially, you're trying to determine what organizations and individuals are relevant to determining the winner. This includes the decision authority, evaluators, stakeholders, and influencers, and don't forget the contract shop! Start with the organization chart for the acquiring organization and facilitate an influence mapping session to identify primary and secondary influencers. Add them to the call plan along with who from your team should make the visit.

Your call plan needs to continually evolve and, remember, this is not just about formal calls at the office. This could be meeting someone at a conference/seminar/workshop/charity event. This could be working with them on an article. This could be talking to them about a very different project you're supporting or has their interest. This could be getting a teammate to initiate the introduction—be creative! If none of the options above work, you need to identify alternatives. And there are times when you are being shut out. You're finding you can't get in and get known. Often those signs lead you to shut down the capture (no bid).

When you have existing work with the customer, your call plan should also include any contract reviews for ongoing work. Talking about future vision, and about the interrelationship of your project with others (including the one you're going after) can yield gold for capture.

If successful, your calls on those involved with the acquisition should provide a reason for a follow-up call. This follow-up call needs to be added to the call plan. Many of your calls will result in identification of other people or organizations who need to be contacted. They need to be added to the call plan.

Using a Contact Report

The contact report helps you prepare for the meeting, and then document the results of executing the call plan. Some basic information is filled in before each meeting (info from the call plan), and then it is used to document the results of the meeting.

As soon as the meeting is scheduled, assign one of your team's attendees the responsibility to prepare and coordinate the contact report. The additional information includes questions to get your contact talking and get information you want, including their perceptions of the project.

Playing the Contractor Game to Win _____

Name/title / Acquisition Role	Contact Info	Likes/ dislikes/ biases	Who	Supporting information & materials needed	Date Due	Completed
		L:				
		D:				
		B:				

Supporting information shared and materials used:

Questions asked:

Notes:

Next Steps:

148

Call preparations

The stated purpose of a meeting needs to be succinct and specific to that visit. Your team's attendees need to decide among themselves who is responsible for delivering each message and who is responsible for asking which question(s). However, it is important to keep the conversation feeling comfortable. You prepare the questions in advance to prepare yourselves and to think about open-ended questions to get the conversation going.

Listen closely to answers and **respond** to where your customer is going. Be interested—be curious—about what they say. Then ask questions based on their responses. Remember your prepared questions are only a guide but not an exact map of how to move forward in the meeting. Stay focused on the customer's answers to ensure your customer knows you're really listening to them. This shows you care about their ideas and perceptions.

Once your attendees agree on their roles, they need to assign someone to take notes. This suggests every call should involve at least two people, as it's hard for one person both to engage the contact in conversation and take notes. Often, it's more effective when the same person doesn't deliver all the messages or ask all the questions. By spreading the responsibility around, you can engage everyone in the conversation and make it seem more natural. There are times when only one of you has a special relationship with the contact, or something happens and only one person attends the meeting. If that's the case, you should take sparing notes allowing you to recall the important details later. This allows you to focus on the conversation. Then as soon as the call is completed, document the details that could be important.

Consult—don't sell

Whenever you communicate with customers, edit out everything that sounds like a high-pressured sales pitch (e.g., emphasizing your standard offering), avoid unsubstantiated claims (e.g., "we have the highest quality"), and avoid marketing hyperbole (e.g., "world class"). Instead, use your interactions to solicit what problems they are trying to solve and the outcomes most important to them. Generally, they will tell you what they need. This may not be expressed as explicit requirements; rather, it may be expressed as problems they face or concerns about the future. You should be prepared to share what has worked for your other clients—what similar problem they faced, what you did, and what were the positive results/outcomes (their problem, your solution, their result - PSR). Or share some exciting new project you're working on that has technology or a process of interest. Conversations are two-way streets—be prepared with information important to your client. When you approach each meeting with a genuine interest in the customer's needs, you'll be surprised with how candid and insightful the answers are. Be curious and be open. Follow their lead while not losing track of what you need to win.

Documenting your meeting

Your attendees should try to meet as soon as possible following the visit to review the notes, compare recollections, identify major takeaways, agree on results/findings, record action items, and define follow-up steps. This information should be documented by the attendee responsible for the contact report and then circulated among the attendees to make it sure it captures the relevant information and represents a consensus of what was learned.

While the contact report is most often used in conjunction with a visit identified in the call plan, it should be prepared whenever a customer contact provides information potentially useful to the capture team. So if you're doing work for the customer on another project, and during a meeting you uncover useful information—make sure you share that. The contact report is a great way to ensure you document any information you learn.

For unexpected meetings (e.g., when SMEs or other capture team members run into clients), take good notes, share information, ask questions, and follow up if something is not clear. Don't let the process get in the way of capturing good intel!

Remember, this is all about learning about the requirements of the procurement!

By talking to those within the client organization and identifying the problems as they see them, you can potentially influence their vision, and you can also make sure your solution matches their vision. If you identify requirements that are overly restrictive or vague, you can engage in value-add discussions to influence the procurement to either protect your incumbency or go after this new piece of work. Ideally this can help you propose a solution meeting **both** the stated requirements and the customer's real need. Remember, your principal objective is to listen and identify their biases and their perceptions. In the world of capture **the truth is no defense against your client's perceptions**.

How To Inspire The Client

What to avoid

"Trust me, your majesty. We're only one 90-pound pigeon from total air control."

When preparing and executing your call plan, **DO NOT**:

- Stop updating it—you'll be surprised how many times your team will have to go back to refresh their memory about who was contacted, when, or by whom.
- Believe this is a one and done—the number of touches matters.
- Let your team make a visit without identifying the purpose, messages, and questions in advance—any attendee who does not agree to this should be excluded (even company executives, including your president).
- Allow attendees to provide just a verbal debrief and not a contact report—the information needs to be captured in writing for future reference.
- Ever use the contact report as a script—meetings are intended to stimulate a dialogue, and you need to be responsive to the conversation and focus on the advances you're looking for; spontaneity and curiosity drive conversations.

- Force or recite the messages—they should come out naturally during the conversation so you can see the reaction of the customer and demonstrate you have fully embraced the ideas.
- Send the questions to the customer attendee ahead of time or hand them to the customer at the start of the meeting—if requested, provide an agenda without the questions. Sending questions in advance takes away the two-sided nature of the conversation.
- Rely on calls made as part of general business development or contract reviews—your opportunity is at best a secondary objective of those reviews and often does not get covered during the meeting. However, contract reviews can be a great time to uncover future vision— prepare for how you can use what you learn there for the capture!

Chapter 16
Getting the Money Right

The best solution in the world will not win if the price is not within the customer's budget.

The cheapest price will not win unless the proposal is acceptable.

The best value at other than the cheapest price might win, if your proposal provides the best value in the eyes of the evaluation team and it's within their budget.

"I told you not to go hard sell."

Influencing and understanding price as a variable

If you're early enough in the game, you can potentially influence the customer's acquisition strategy, the way price will be evaluated, and possibly even the budget itself. To do so, you need to understand how much power the client has with regard to the funding source, how important cost is in selecting the winner, and what the competition is likely to bid. This requires continual research and analysis on client behavior, the behavior of your competition, and behavior/changes in the market. You also need to know the influence of all of those within the client organization and what influence your competition may have with the client organization. Answer these questions:

- Who has this as a must win?
- What does the behavior of the client and the competition tell you?
- Where has the client stood with regard to weighing price against best value, in the last year?

To get this right, you need information on the customer organization's acquisition history to determine how price plays into their selection decisions. You need information on your competition's bidding experience to determine how they are likely to bid in this case. You then use this information to formulate recommendations to the customer as to what best allows them to meet their objectives and provide a competitive acquisition.

For long captures, make sure you stay current with the field—organizations change. Change impacts the decision-makers and decision making as regards to the elements affecting cost and price.

Price to win

Put your PTW hat on. As capture manager, you need to identify what you think the winning price is. This is based on client preferences (e.g., technology used, staffing approach, schedule) and what the competition will propose. Calculating PTW is not something you do alone. It needs to be done with your management, members of your capture team, and your pricing staff. There are several consulting firms that provide PTW analysis support if you lack the expertise in-house.

The PTW is an estimate developed specifically for each opportunity. Start by establishing upper and lower limits on what your data indicate the customer is likely to pay (see Figure 1). These are data you need to gather early in the capture process as part of your other information gathering. The upper limit is the price above which your bid exceeds the budget. The minimum is the price below which the customer determines the risk of performance is too high, materially unbalanced, or violates known (e.g., Service Contract Act, collective bargaining agreements) or perceived constraints. Base your PTW on publicly available data—no dumpster diving! You can use past contract awards and reverse engineering to derive rates and markups. You should use the competition's most likely approach (which may be different from yours) to estimate their price. The result is your best guess of where your price needs to be to justify selection of your offer.

How To Inspire The Client

Competitive Edge

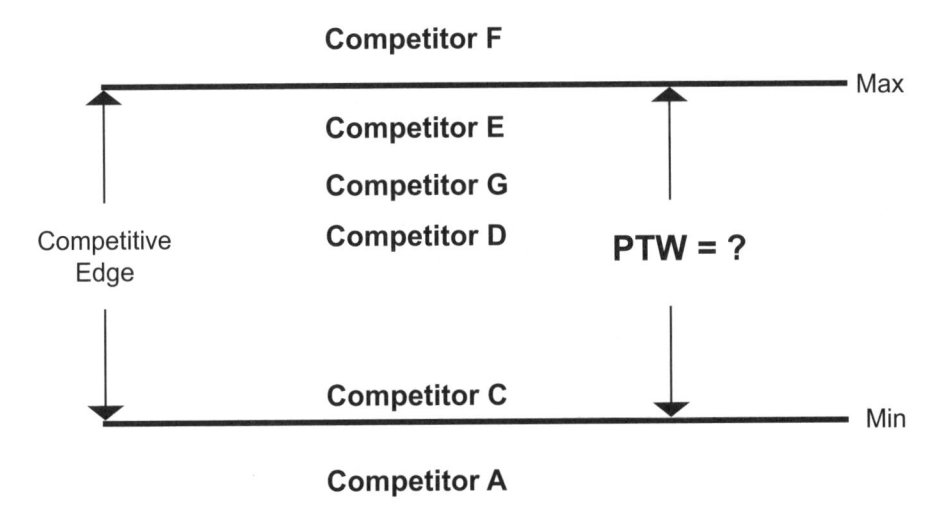

Competitor F
Competitor E
Competitor G
Competitor D
Competitor C
Competitor A

PTW = ?

Max
Min

Figure 1. Setting the Price to Win.

Pricing strategy

Your responsibility as capture manager is to provide the customer an offer they can't refuse. Such an offer requires the right combination of technical, management, and cost elements. If you work the cost solution at the same time as you're working the technical and management solutions, the proposal process is less painful, and your product will be better. For example, you select teammates that can meet the pricing objectives and your technical solution is consistent with your price to win.

Unless the work is LPTA (Lowest Price Technically Acceptable) or you know this client always only picks the lowest price, pricing strategies and PTW are NOT about the lowest price—they are about the right PTW. Pricing strategies are needed to help you get there. Your pricing strategy factors into your technical, management and cost solutions. It impacts everything, from your teaming strategy to the benefits you give employees.

Here are some ideas to consider as you develop your pricing strategy:

Only price what is requested—not what you think they want. Make that clear with your assumptions—and make sure your assumptions are in line with what the customer is asking.

If the cost evaluation is based on pricing labor categories, look for ways to use the evaluation model to your advantage. For example:

- give fewer hours to more expensive categories;
- bid zero hours in labor categories you won't use (you need to know what will be acceptable to the client);
- use market survey data to justify rates lower than the incumbent is currently paying;
- If a multi-year contract, start with more senior people and move in more junior people once the program is up and running and that level of experience is no longer needed;
- identify work that lends itself to use of lower-cost subcontractors; or
- identify new processes or technology that gets the work done at a lower cost (need to be able to verify that).

Creating a good cost proposal

Your job as capture manager is to make sure the cost proposal is addressed with the same rigor as other elements of the overall solution. It is not something separate created in a back room. It must correctly reflect what is described in the technical and management sections and justify why it is the right price for this work. There are three parts to developing a good cost proposal: **PTW**, **BOE** (Basis of Estimate), and **bottoms-up cost estimate**. Generally, the PTW is done early in the capture process. The BOE and bottoms-up estimate are developed as you have sufficient detail about your solution. The solution should be driven by the PTW. Figure 2 illustrates the relationship between the PTW and the bottoms-up estimate.

The **PTW** is driven by the competition and what the customer thinks the price should be. It should put downward pressure to balance the upward pressure that is likely to come from your bottoms-up estimate (see Figure 2).

The **BOE** is the documentation allowing you and the customer to understand and assess your costs. It is the rationale for the cost of each of the elements of your proposed cost. As each solicitation is different in terms of what information is required with the cost proposal, your solicitation may not explicitly require a BOE. Even if it doesn't, your team should prepare a BOE to document the proposed costs and serve as a check on your calculations. This becomes valuable later during negotiations and final proposal revisions.

The **bottoms-up estimate** identifies the cost of all the individual elements of your solution. It includes management reserve and profit.

PTW
- *Market and competitor driven*
- *Sets the target based on customer affordability and competitor dynamics*

- *Internally driven*
- *Focus on BOEs and consistency between technical and management volumes*

Bottoms-up Estimate

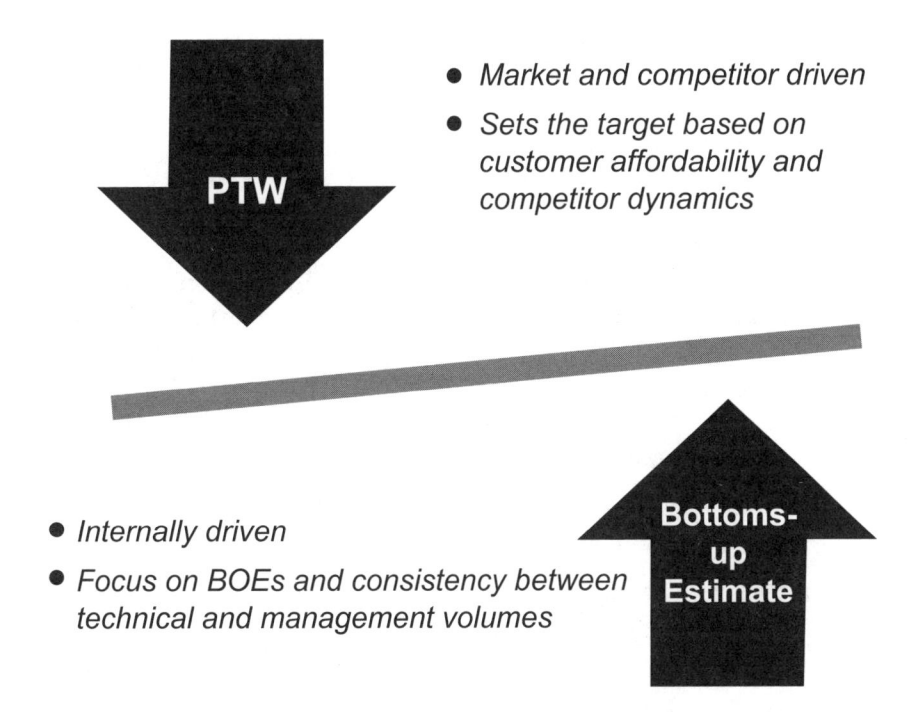

Figure 2: Striking the appropriate balance for the winning price.

Tools for costing

As the PTW is a top-down estimate of what your price needs to be, it does not presuppose a solution. The BOE and bottoms-up estimate are based on your team's solution. Often, the three elements do not agree. If your bottoms-up cost estimate is too high, assume your solution is too expensive and start identifying ways to lower the cost. The tools available to you as capture manager to get your price to the PTW from the bottoms-up estimate include:

- adjusting your proposed solution;
- keeping your solution and accepting the risk of achieving lower the cost; or
- convincing management to accept less profit.

Use the BOE to document decisions made on how to achieve the proposed price.

WARNING! You need to determine whether your solution is too expensive as early as possible and, if it is, work on ways to lower the cost. This is necessary because you need to maintain a close connection between your solution and its price. Last minute cost-cutting exercises and pricing changes introduce inconsistencies, inaccuracies, and false claims. And trying to make such changes at a late stage can risk your ability to maintain your close coordination with both corporate management and the key personnel who will be performing the work.

How To Inspire The Client

Questions about your clients

Use the questions on this page and the next two pages to help you develop your cost solution:

- Client:
    - What do you know about the client's budget?
    - How accurately do you know the client's budget?
    - What role does cost play for this client?
    - Where is the client in relation to what they want in terms of capability vs cost?
    - Where is the client moving in relation to considering price-based versus technical-based on decisions during the past year?
    - Where does the client see value AND where is your competition in relation to being able to offer perceived value?
    - Where are you on the tradeoffs?
    - What is the client's posture with regard to potential changes?
        - Are they under pressure for change?
        - Do they change contractors?
        - Do they go with lower price?
    - If this is a follow-on contract:
        - How much of the current budget has been spent?
        - What changes have there been in scope, staffing mix, or labor categories?
        - Has there been a change in budget?
        - Has the customer expressed interest in changes?

Questions about your competition

- What companies have shown an interest?
- What do you know about how your competition will price this and the techniques they may use to get the price down?
- If this is a follow-on contract (including yours):
  - What changes have there been in the client organization?
  - How long has the incumbent held the contract(s)?
  - How often has the prime contractor changed?
  - How critical is this program to the incumbent (i.e., what will they do to keep it)?
  - What, if any, publicity has there been about the work?
  - How stable has the contract been (review the incumbent's hiring for this contract)?
  - Who bid last time and how did they do?
  - What new competitors and teams might you face?

Questions about your solution

- Can you do any of the work differently from the way it is being done now (e.g., can you use automation to perform the work with 10 FTEs (Full Time Equivalents) instead of the current 15)?
- How can you adjust your solution for better financials and lower cost?
- If this would be a takeaway, what are the transition costs, and can you offer transition at no cost to the customer (as an investment)?
- What are the transition risks and costs (rebadge, new hire, combo)?
- What will it take to beat the incumbent on price?
- If you're the incumbent, what it would take to beat you, and will the competition do that? Profit? Staffing? Facilities? Tools? Etc.?

Playing the Contractor Game to Win

Chapter 17
Developing Solutions Your Client Can Get Excited About

"We checked the rulebook and there's nothing about insole thickness."

Getting to a winning solution, the solution this client selects, is your primary job. You're the person who must be continually focused on what it takes to win. What it takes to win is a compelling and convincing narrative, clearly articulated win themes, and the solution that the client wants.

The winning solution shows the client you understand their needs and how to make them successful within their budget. As we discuss throughout the book, you want to develop ideas and vet them within the client organization prior to release of the solicitation. You want to get their feedback. You want to know how they articulate their needs and their vision for the solution. Then you want to use their exact words. In the best of all possible worlds, they see themselves in the solution you present in your proposal, as they have discussed it with you and had input into your approach.

At the appropriate times in your capture, bring in creative types from across your organization, from across the team you have established, and from the outside. They help you get new ideas flowing and bring innovation to your solution.

Aligning what you're selling with the solution they're buying

Solution development is often the most difficult and time-consuming step in the capture process. It requires research, diligence, intellect, and attention to detail. By solution, we mean all the elements required to win. This includes the technical and management approaches, your team, your price, and your past performance references (see Chapter 21). Your job as capture manager is to ensure all the pieces reinforce each other in a logical and consistent manner.

Capture is about people, not analytical techniques. We haven't yet found any analytical techniques that replace the need for a diverse capture team (e.g., highly technical personnel, personnel familiar with the customer, personnel familiar with your company's capabilities) working together. Identifying a solution that aligns with what is important to the customer is all that matters.

Large companies frequently have designated solution architects. In smaller companies, this role often falls to the capture manager. Regardless of who fills the role, your proposal must combine a solution that is perceived as being superior to your competitors with compelling communication to describe how your solution will make the client successful.

Critical Knowledge for Good Solutioning

Before launching into solutioning, spend some time synthesizing the information you've collected so far. The following questions are intended to help that process:

- What outcomes does the customer want most from this contract?
- How does the customer define success?
- Which requirements does the customer consider most important?
- For what, if anything, is the customer is willing to pay extra?
- Are there requirements on which the customer is willing to compromise?
- What preferences/biases does the customer have about the way in which the requirements are met (methods, processes, staffing, tools)?
- What price is the customer willing and able to pay?
- What is the competition likely to bid as their solution?
- Will the skill types and levels be dictated or are you free to propose a solution based on only the solicitation requirements?

Getting ready for solutioning

No matter what the customer is buying, their decision will be based on an evaluation of your proposed solution. This is true whether the contract is to develop a new financial management system, implement a call center, help them run a specific program, or augment their staff. Defining your solution needs to start very early in the capture. A winning solution requires you to do a lot of work prior to release of either the draft or final solicitation and well before the customer imposes the cone of silence.

Have your solutioning team start by analyzing the requirements you have gathered to understand how your solution might be evaluated. If this is an existing contract, you have the last set of requirements and evaluation criteria as a starting point. If this is new work, find similar work, if you can, to identify what the likely evaluation criteria will be. Then use what you learned from your capture activities to hone your understanding of what the customer needs and wants today.

Developing your solution
Solutioning teams often resist working out the details during capture before they see a solicitation, as well as when the solicitation has significant page limitations, involves only an oral presentation, or doesn't include an evaluation of your implementation approach. Your job is to get your SMEs to work through the details of the solution, one that provides the features necessary to meet all contract requirements, even if you don't need to address them all in the proposal.

Your need to push your SMEs to provide sufficient details to determine solution elements, including appropriate methodology (e.g., agile, iterative, waterfall), approach (e.g., flows that show integration of client approvals), required staffing (e.g., knowledge, skills, numbers), organizational structure (e.g., functional, product teams, customer facing), and pricing (e.g., staff, travel, tools, infrastructure). This is the level that allows you to develop the BOE.

The details matter, no matter what! These details allow you to have appropriate discussions with your client, identify aspects that exceed contract requirements, highlight elements that reduce implementation risk, and avoid a proposal that sounds arrogant and boastful or provides a motorcycle when they wanted a bicycle. Getting these details right, though not easy, is necessary to identify whether your solution aligns with the customer's needs, wants, and budget, or if you need to make changes.

Push your team to answer these questions:

- What product will be developed or service delivered as a result of your actions?
- How do you intend to implement your solution?
- What is required and what would be "nice to haves" of the solution?
- What are the required inputs?
- What are the specific steps/actions—what is the work flow and who is involved at each step?
- What are the required interfaces (technical, client, regulatory)?
- What are the required tools, and what does the client already have?
- What are the required government-furnished items, including office space (if applicable)?
- Are there easier, less costly ways to meet the requirements (e.g., what were the tradeoffs and why did you pick this solution)?

Draw Your Solution

Displaying your solution with a combination of graphics and bullets will ease the anxiety of staring at a blank screen and trying to compose text for most of your solution teams. It focuses your efforts on the essential content, identifies areas that may need additional focus, and ensures your solution is based on the actual client needs and not just your company's offering.

Your graphics can include flow diagrams, timelines, client interaction diagrams, organizational charts, and/or screen shots. Allow your SMEs to use whatever techniques they prefer (e.g., shared whiteboard that can be virtual, each person going off and documenting their ideas and coming back together to share, using a graphic artist while the team discusses the solution—anything that works for your team) to mature their thinking and document your solution.

Just like your solutioning team members, different evaluators absorb and process information in various ways. Share a description of elements of your solution with the client and notice their reactions. Allow them to provide tangible feedback on what you share and discuss their proposed changes. Then take the changes back to the team. When the client sees their input in your proposal, they'll know and appreciate you listened and paid attention to their concerns—and the chances you will win will go up.

Winning solution

Your goal is to address the customer's needs in ways that score higher than your competition—this is how you win. In scoring, most clients use some type of relative comparison of your proposed solution against the source selection criteria. They then compare scores to determine the winner. Most solicitations describe the scoring method, the evaluation factors, and how the winner is selected. **Remember, scoring is subjective**, so something that is new and different that you have not socialized with the client, even if it hits every evaluation criterion, will not necessarily score higher.

In a best-value competition, the scoring is based on significant strengths, strengths, deficiencies, significant weaknesses, and risks. For this scoring system, your objective is to score only significant strengths and strengths with no weaknesses, deficiencies, or risks.

The Lohfeld Consulting Group has a five-part definition of what constitutes a strength. It is a feature not neutralized by other bidders (i.e., becomes a discriminator for your bid) and provides one or more of the following benefits from your customer's viewpoint (ideally validated by the customer prior to the cone of silence):

1. Exceeds a contract requirement.
2. Significantly increases likelihood of successful contract performance.
3. Significantly increases the likelihood of successful mission accomplishment.
4. Provides something the customer would pay extra to receive.
5. Mitigates mission or contract risk.

Once you know the evaluation criteria attributes, you can tailor your solution to address them, using information from conversations with the client to develop your narrative of how this will work for them. This will help you achieve the goal of meeting all customer requirements (being fully compliant) and earn a high score because your solution addresses both their written and unwritten concerns and biases. For example, if the evaluation criteria state the client will score the *efficiency* and *effectiveness* of your organizational structure, you will know how they define efficient and effective as they relate to the outcomes they want—if you have done capture well.

Quick/Cheap/Quality—Pick 2
Every solution involves tradeoffs. The big ones are often where customer input is needed. Don't expect the customer to make the decision for you, so don't put them in a position that sounds like you're asking them to pick an option. Instead, use customer meetings to discuss the tradeoffs, the potential alternatives, and the criteria for selecting a course of action. Their reactions help you determine what alternatives they have considered, whether they agree with your selection criteria, and what they consider the most important aspects of the solution. Such discussions open the customer to your thought processes, considerations they might not have thought about, and how your solution best addresses their immediate and future needs. You also might identify certain biases they have that you have yet to address. Use the input you receive from the client or stakeholders to sharpen the way you present your solution. Often the tradeoff criteria can be used to describe the benefits of your specific solution. For you to win, the customer must perceive your proposal as providing the best solution for this program.

How To Inspire The Client

"Here you go—that'll be $47.50"

Convincing Solutions Answer the Question: "So What?"
As your team works to define the solution they intend to propose, you continually need to ask *SO WHAT?* The answer describes what happens if your solution is implemented. The answer needs to be expressed from the customer's perspective; what they need and value. This requires you to know what they want. Challenge your team to describe:

- how your solution meets the client's stated requirements, from conversations and/or the solicitation;
- what benefits they can expect; and
- how it enables them to meet their future aspirations.

To provide a solution that goes beyond how the customer articulates the requirements to where they see project success, use a feature/benefit/proof construct to keep your discussions focused on the customer. Clearly identify the features that can be scored as a strength and make sure you can articulate the benefit *to this customer.* Sometimes you can show how your proposed solution increases the likelihood of successful contract performance/mission performance, or even exceed the contract requirements, while meeting your PTW. Your solution may also incorporate a feature that reduces risks. Risks and weaknesses are closely related. By describing features to reduce risk, you're also eliminating potential weaknesses. During conversations with the customer, you can find out what risks they are most concerned about and what resonates with whom within their organization.

The capture process is necessary so you can develop and provide conclusions for the evaluators they consider positive. In the proposal stage, you need to provide the evaluators with your own strong, supported conclusions. Don't make the evaluators work to develop their own—and potentially incorrect—conclusions. You need your solutioning team to have developed the proof to substantiate the benefits of a proposed feature. Without proof, your claims are merely unsubstantiated assertions that will not be scored or might be seen as a weakness.

> **WARNING!** *Tailoring the solution to the evaluation criteria alone, while ignoring or not focusing sufficiently on contract requirements, has often led to proposals being judged as being non-responsive or having significant weaknesses. First and foremost, your solution needs to be compliant with the contract requirements, and once you have done that, the proposal becomes a packaging exercise. Have your solutioning team answer these questions:*
> - *What feature of your solution meets each evaluation criterion?*
> - *What contract requirements drove the solution?*
> - *What are the challenges associated with implementing your solution?*

Three types of solutions

The following pages provide you with descriptions of three types of solutions. They're listed in the recommended order of preference. Because your final solution has multiple aspects (e.g., technical, management, price) and each of those aspects has multiple parts, your final solution will likely combine elements of all three types:

1. A solution successfully implemented by your company or a team member on another relevant contract.
2. A solution based on industry (or customer) best practices.
3. A solution based on a new or innovative idea.

If the customer expresses preferences for a solution not included in these three solution types, your only opportunity to influence their thinking is prior to release of the final solicitation. In discussing your solution, you need to describe its relevance to the requirements and how you intend to implement it. This includes details about the inputs, activities, and tools you intend to use. You need to walk away with your client's biases/preferences and those biases must be reflected in your solution.

How To Inspire The Client

Solution type 1

A solution successfully implemented by your company or a team member on another relevant contract. In using this type of solution, you need to describe the following:

- Why the previous contract is relevant, including the problem(s) solved, and relevant features of the solution.
- How you intend to adapt that solution to this customer's unique requirements.
- Specific examples from the previous contract (proof the solution worked, the benefits that customer experienced, and benefits this customer can expect).

As it is easier to describe your solution in a compelling, convincing, and credible manner when you refer to actual results on a relevant contract, the preferred solution type is one based on what your company has previously implemented. Using success stories from another contract captures the evaluator's attention, demonstrates an understanding of how to implement the solution, and substantiates your claims about potential benefits.

An efficient way to introduce the basis for your proposed solution is to use the problem-solution-result (PSR) format. You briefly describe the previous customer's problem (relating it as closely as possible to the current solicitation requirements), how you overcame the problem (your solution), and the results achieved (expressed as customer benefits meaningful to the new customer). See how they respond—do they find it interesting, do they have questions, etc.?

Proposing this type of solution requires your team to research what your company/team member has done before. They need to identify which previous contracts had similar requirements, what your solution was, and how it addressed that customer's needs. This doesn't mean you should just describe how great you were in the past. You could describe how you're going to use that experience to address the new customer's requirements. It should be about the client's needs. You should also analyze the previous job to determine the elements that are different, as well. Anticipate how the previous contract may not be viewed as applicable to the current solicitation, and be prepared to explain why this experience can be viewed as relevant and appropriate lessons learned.

Solution type 2

A solution based on industry (or customer) best practices. In using this type of solution, you need to describe the following:

- Why the relevant best practices are applicable to this customer's unique requirements.
- How you intend to use these best practices to meet the customer's specific requirements.
- Your team's prior experience implementing best practices (not necessarily the specific best practices being addressed in this solution).
- Representative examples of the benefits this customer can expect (proof that the best practices solution works, and the benefits customers have experienced).

A best practices solution is usually adopted to reduce implementation risk or because the customer has expressed a preference for an established, recognized solution. A solution based on best practices is strongest when your company has implemented those specific practices on a prior contract (see solution type 1). Even if your company does not have this experience, your proposal can still be successful if you have key personnel from the team who do have such experience. Or you have other experience you can demonstrate as being comparable—and directly relevant—to what the client is looking for.

Remember, in this type of solution, compliance with the best practices is the central feature of your solution and not the benefit. Describe the benefits in terms of the value to the customer. When writing/describing your solution, your team needs to research thoroughly the relevant best practices and understand the types of situations where they have been implemented, both successfully and unsuccessfully. This enables your team to explain to the client how you propose to implement the best practices, how and where those best practices have been used effectively, and how to avoid difficulties encountered in other situations (avoiding previous failures). If the use of best practices has caused problems, you will need to show the client you know about those problems and have ways to mitigate them.

Solution type 3

A solution based on a new or innovative idea. In using this type of solution, you need to describe the following:

- Why the customer's requirements do not lend themselves to a previously employed solution or best practice.
- Why your "good idea" is the preferred solution (in terms directly relevant to the customer's needs and wants).
- How you intend to implement this solution.
- Why the customer should have confidence the solution will work, and the benefits will be realized.

Unfortunately, many teams too quickly gravitate to this type of solution ("Here's a good idea!"). Clients want to be comfortable with your solution. It helps their comfort level, especially if they're risk adverse, when you can demonstrate you've done this before and been successful with it. So don't let your solutioning team fall into the "new idea" trap. You need to be able to explain why a previous solution doesn't meet the customer's requirements and how yours does.

To prevent your innovative solution from being dismissed out of hand, try to have one of your SMEs meet with the client to discuss your ideas and see how they respond. This may help you to turn it into a superior solution by tailoring it to meet the client's perceptions of what is feasible and what is too risky.

How To Inspire The Client

Even when you use a new idea solution in conjunction with another solution type, the burden for your solutioning team is make the client see the new idea as a real and viable approach. It can't merely <u>sound</u> like a good idea. It needs to be both tangible and scoreable.

Your solutioning team needs to be able to identify how your solution exceeds requirements, increases the likelihood of success, and mitigates risk. And because it is a new idea, you likely have no substantial track record on which to base these determinations. So your explanations and support need to be well-thought-out, concise, and convincing.

Testing your solution

In the best of all possible worlds, the customer sees themselves implementing the solution you present in your proposal—and it is the solution they want. One method of getting there is to test aspects of your solution—key personnel, technology, processes—with the customer in advance to get their reaction. This is not a one-time or one-person activity. You need to create multiple opportunities to gather first-hand feedback so you can figure out what the customer wants in their solution. This includes both their immediate needs and future aspirations.

You'll only have a limited number of opportunities to test your ideas with the customer, so don't expect to discuss every detail. Whether you get meetings during regular business hours or get the opportunity to discuss ideas at a conference or other gathering, include these meetings in your capture calendar and use the time you get carefully and efficiently.

Testing your solution with the client doesn't mean you make a presentation explicitly describing what you intend to propose. Prepare and maximize the time by focusing on the elements of your solution that can differentiate you. It should be a conversation where you discuss pieces of your proposed solution from the perspective of the client. For technology or process ideas, come prepared to talk about what you've done to meet the needs of other similar customers. And be prepared with open-ended questions to determine their interest in those types of solutions and whether they can help solve what they see as their problem/issue.

Be ready with examples of the successes your customers have had with the proposed solution. Describe the previous customer's requirements in terms directly relevant to this customer. Then describe the approach you used to solve them and the results achieved. The results need to be described in terms of the *benefits the previous customer experienced*. Be ready to respond if the customer begins asking questions about elements of your solution. Think proactively and offer the customer suggestions about how others have solved similar problems. This shows them you're thinking about them. It also lets you better understand the context of their problem and how you can incorporate their thoughts of viable solutions into your proposed solution.

You should start to work your solution early in the capture process. If you are the incumbent, NEVER suggest something new right before a recompete or in your proposal. You need to do that at least one year in advance so it doesn't appear to be solely in response to wanting to win again. If you are not an incumbent, you still need to start work on your solution well before release of the solicitation. In either situation, be sure to test aspects of your solution often, with final discussions as close to the RFP release date as possible.

Ideally you will know with whom you will be testing your solution, and whether they are likely to share your information with others. You may have concerns about competitors getting to see your material. If you are not the incumbent, or if you are intending to propose something the customer may not yet be considering, you need to give the customer an advance look of enough of your solution it won't come as a surprise in your proposal. Also, you should be careful to send or leave behind only materials you would not mind finding their way to a competitor. Remember the reason you are sharing materials with the client is to help you to tailor your solution for them, not to help your competitors to do the same.

Using members of the delivery team
As much as possible, use members of the delivery team when testing your solution with the customer. This allows the customer to interact with members of your team with whom they will be working in the future. Your objective is to build their confidence in your people and your work—to allow the client to envision how you intend to implement your solution and provide them with value. Meetings between your delivery team and the client can sometimes be scheduled formally or they can be set up quite informally, especially if SMEs already have ongoing contacts/relationships with people within the client organization. Be creative.

Asking the right questions
Solutioning is not like taking an order. You can't expect to merely ask the customer what they want and have them describe it in detail. Government customers often don't know exactly what they want or what alternatives exist, especially early in the process. They usually are focused on the business or operational problem they are trying to solve. Even if they know what they want, they may not be allowed to tell you anything about how to solve their problem or provide specific feedback on your solution. This means you need to ask the right questions to figure out the details of what they are looking for, and to determine what you must offer to meet their objectives and expectations. Chapter 9 (previously) identifies many of the questions you need to ask—and answer—in the process of defining the opportunity and developing aspects of your solution.

Using internal reviews
Use internal reviews to test concepts and prepare for customer interactions. These internal peer and solution reviews (sometimes called "murder boards") provide the opportunity to test your ideas and ensure they are responding to the customer's requirements. Don't think of these reviews as a burden. Instead use them to your advantage. Insist the reviewers include one or more people who are familiar with the customer and their objectives, others who are familiar with your team's experience on related contracts, and still others who are familiar with your potential and actual competitors. Use this group of internal reviewers to help you determine which elements of your potential solution are already known and which ones need customer input.

Providing a solution that outscores the competition

A winning solution provides the evaluation team with a clear picture of what they are buying. This starts with an overview of the features and how they meet the customers' needs and wants. The presentation of your solution to the client should clearly answer these questions:

- How do the features of your solution meet the evaluation criteria attributes? This is compliance.
- What efficiencies or improvements does your solution provide that they will experience as benefits?
- Which features of your solution, if any, exceed a contract requirement in a way the client will perceive as providing value while staying within their budget?
- How does your solution increase the likelihood of successful contract/mission performance?
- How does your solution minimize risk?
- What makes your solution unique?
- How is your solution different and better than the competition's?
- How is the resulting product or service better than the one proposed by a competitor?
- What are the challenges/drawbacks of other solutions (ghosting the competition)?

Preparing for the evaluators

Helping the evaluators get it

Evaluators have a short attention span and limited tolerance for complex solutions. They only want to have to read enough to reach their decision. The evaluation team should be able to find a clear mapping between the solicitation requirements and features of your solution. So, during your pre-proposal capture efforts, the capture team needs to:

1. Describe your solution in ways both technical and non-technical people can easily and quickly understand.
2. Ensure the evaluator can easily navigate your proposal and find the information to score.
3. Use the customer's own words when describing your solution.
4. Translate abstract/ambiguous terms (e.g., approach, understanding, capabilities) into concrete terms (e.g., inputs, actions, experience).
5. Avoid word-drop modifiers and superlatives—don't use evaluation attributes as a modifier when describing your solution. Use "Our solution ..." not "Our effective and efficient solution ..."). Such superlatives lack substantiation and decrease credibility.
6. Describe the benefits/value of your solution in ways the customer will find meaningful.
7. Support claims with facts. Quantify the facts whenever possible.
8. Don't write about anything the evaluator doesn't care about. This is a mistake even good writers make. As capture manager, make every sentence earn its place in the proposal.

For instance, in the management section of the proposal, you should answer questions such as the following:

- What are the specific elements of your organizational structure (based on what the client cares about)?
- Where have you used this organizational structure before to achieve results similar to what this client wants/needs?
- What made it effective on the previous contract?
- How does your organizational structure improve the likelihood of meeting this customer's requirements?
- Have you evaluated alternative organizational structures with which your client has had experience, and can you show how and why yours will result in stronger outcomes?
- Why is your selected organizational structure the most efficient?

Section 5
Your Role Once the Solicitation Drops

As we said earlier, once a draft or final solicitation drops, you are usually prohibited from communicating with personnel within the client organization, except through questions sent to the Contracting Officer/Contracting Specialists/Procurement Office.

However capture most definitely does not stop. In addition to the important continuing role you'll play in developing a winning proposal, you need to continue to be aware of meetings and events, and you need to keep abreast of client and competitor websites and social media. And make sure your own website is up-to-date. Find ways to keep your name/brand out in front in positive ways if you can. Be creative.

CHAPTER 18
DRAFT SOLICITATION

Some clients provide one or more draft solicitations. They generally do so to improve the quality of their ultimate solicitation and give you time to get started on your proposal. Take advantage of these opportunities to provide valuable feedback on the solicitation and improve your solution.

As capture manager, your primary roles are threefold:

- *Reviewer* to see if there are any red flags—has someone influenced the solicitation in a way you didn't expect or created a problem for your team and/or solution?
- *Author* of the Introduction/Executive Summary and messaging for each section.
- *Partner* for the Proposal Manager to ensure they get the support they need, including from you.

If you do find red flags, you need to determine how much risk they pose to your win probability and how to address them. Do not hide any of them—conduct a formal review with those people you need who can help. Use them to figure out your responses and then execute the plan of action.

By this point in the process, you have gathered considerable information on the client. You know much about how they define success, both personally and for the program/project, and the "as is" environment. You also have learned some of the client's personal and organizational biases and expectations. And you have gotten to meet with and know influential people in the client organization. As soon as you have the draft solicitation, you can use it to determine how to turn this information into an effective proposal—one that continues your conversations with the customer by addressing their needs, concerns, and preferences.

Your work, as capture manager, includes outlining the introduction/executive summary. It needs to be about the client, not about you. It should show you understand their challenges (why this solicitation matters to them), identify the barriers they face; and then summarize your story by clearly setting out the benefits. Benefits are the "so whats" the client will gain from your solution (technical, management, and cost). Just complying with the technical requirements isn't enough. State the benefits the way you want the client to see them. This is not about beautiful writing at this point—it is about getting down the ideas that will flow throughout the proposal. Always remember: a proposal is not about you! It's about your client and how you meet their needs.

"Allow me to introduce our new win strategy."

CHAPTER 19
FINAL SOLICITATION

"Now pay attention! Here comes the tricky part!"

The solicitation is finally here! In this phase you have several responsibilities—pay attention to them all:

1. Identifying red flags that could negatively impact your solution or your team.
2. Being the final arbiter of inconsistencies or ambiguities within the solicitation and determining what questions you still need to ask and how to ask them.
3. Validating your value proposition framework.
4. Ensuring you have the right resources, they are deployed correctly, and barriers (e.g., billing, feeding, space, other commitments) to their success are removed.
5. Ensuring your solution and value propositions are accurately reflected throughout all sections of the proposal.
6. Maximizing the effectiveness of your color team reviews.
7. Being the final arbiter of how to respond to color review comments/suggestions.
8. Maintaining your team's relationships and conversations with the client, as possible, during the proposal and up to award (there are ways to legally do this).

Red flags tell you there are important things you did not learn during your information gathering. Among the red flags to be on the lookout for are unanticipated requirements (potentially influenced by one or more of your competitors). Determining the reason for the new requirement will inform your strategy moving forward. Another red flag item would arise if the evaluation criteria you expected from the draft solicitation have been changed significantly in the final solicitation. It potentially means others within the client organization (possibly other than the ones you know) may have influenced changes in the development of the final solicitation or were initiated based on input from one of your competitors.

"This bid is so well done it's like they've been in the room with us!"

Align what you learned with final solicitation

You've spent all this time developing relationships and gathering and analyzing information. And now you need to make sure your proposal reflects the conversations you have been having with the customer organization. Hopefully, you know much more about the client's interests, concerns, and motivations than you did when you started capture. Now that the RFP is here, you can help the authors by:

- validating and revising the introduction/executive summary written during the pre-RFP phase;
- making sure all elements of your proposal match the tone and outline of the RFP;
- confirming and adapting your pre-RFP solution for each section of the proposal still conforms to the proposed requirements; and
- validating and revising your solution to ensure it scores well against the evaluation criteria.

Your role is to ensure the following elements: (1) your story matches what the client is requiring in the final solicitation, (2) your win themes are presented appropriately in each and every section, and (3) you are adequately addressing issues of special concern to the client which may not be obvious from the RFP. Ideally, in viewing your solution, the client should see themselves and what they are looking for. Making sure this happens is your job!

How to make color team reviews most effective

Color team reviews are a necessary and valuable part of the proposal process. You need to help your proposal manager make these reviews effective and improve the quality of the proposal. You should identify who participates in these review teams. You should also help the proposal manager to provide quality material for the reviewers. After the review, you can then help the proposal team to respond to their feedback. Today some companies are implementing an agile model for part or all of the review cycle, which can be effective. Whatever color team process you use, use it to improve your proposal.

Your instructions to the reviewers need to be clear in terms of what is expected of their review. Make sure reviewers receive the solicitation, compliance matrix, and other relevant artifacts days before their review. You and your proposal manager need to provide your review team with detailed guidance about what they need to do to improve the story, the messaging, and the technical content through every section of the proposal. Remember the reviewers may not have the detailed knowledge of the opportunity or customer you do. Provide the review team with the essential knowledge they need to make their review valid.

You need to work with the proposal manager to determine how to respond to color team feedback. You're the arbiter of whether a comment is valid and what resources to apply in addressing suggested changes. Work with the proposal manager to ensure the proposal team understands your decisions and receives clear guidance about how to proceed.

If a color team questions the basic validity or adequacy of your proposed solution, you must make whatever changes are required to ensure the proposal is compliant and complete. After you are sure you have a compliant and complete proposal, a subsequent review needs to confirm it is also compelling and convincing (i.e., it will score well).

CHAPTER 20
GETTING READY TO WRITE

Ideally 60% of your proposal work should occur prior to RFP release, 30% between RFP release and proposal submittal, and 10% after initial submittal. This reflects how important your capture efforts, which are begun well before the release of the final RFP, are to the success of your proposal. Government contracting is very competitive. To win, you need to focus every step of the capture process on gathering and organizing the information you need in order for you to make your proposals and solutions stand out from the competition. The proposal alone is never enough. The groundwork of the capture process is essential to your success.

CHAPTER 21
PAST PERFORMANCE

Past performance is an element of your solution and needs to be treated as such. It should not be considered less important, even if it has less relative importance in terms of the evaluation criteria. We say this because past performance citations are often not developed until after the final solicitation is received and then prepared by members of the staff not directly involved with other elements of the proposal. Past performance citations must be considered as you meet with the customer and develop your solution. Your solution (e.g., technical approach, management approach, and price) must take into consideration what past performance you can cite. Quantifiable performance from your previous experience should be an attribute for each feature of your solution. Customers rarely select a company that can't demonstrate they've done this type of work before.

Past performance citations need to sell your ability and your solution (approach, team, benefits), just like the rest of the proposal. They substantiate the assertions you make about your team's capabilities and the benefits of your solution. Ideally you can find an example of a previous customer who had similar needs as the new customer. You can then show the new customer the benefits the previous customer realized from the solution you are proposing. You don't have to offer exactly the same technology, the same approach, or the same team. You simply need to use the past performance to give the new customer confidence you know what you're talking about and have a track record of solving similar problems.

Your role as capture manager is to lead your capture team as they identify and select relevant past performance citations. You must ensure the past performance section tracks to both the requirements and language in the RFP. You must also confirm they are referenceable accounts. Most solicitations now require past performance customers to complete a questionnaire. You need to ensure the person within the customer organization selected to receive this questionnaire is going to provide a glowing endorsement of your work. This goes for teammate past performance citations as well. We emphasize your responsibility to review and evaluate past performance citations to make sure they are both relevant and helpful to your team. After all, you are the person most knowledgeable about your win strategy, value proposition, win themes, and solution. You need to ensure the color team members reviewing past performances are also evaluating other relevant portions of your proposal so they can assess whether the past performance is both relevant to and supportive of your solution.

Section 6
The Proposal is In—Don't Stop Now

"I'm exhausted – can we pick this up again tomorrow?"

CHAPTER 22
BEST AND FINAL/FINAL PROPOSAL REVISION

Start planning for the Best and Final Offer (BAFO)/Final Proposal Revision (FPR) before the proposal gets submitted. Since lots of time can pass between proposal submission and whatever comes next, make sure to keep your files organized, get contact information for everyone who worked on the various parts of the proposal, and make notes about decisions made along the way that affected your price. Stay in contact with your subcontractors, too. Work through what options you have in terms of potential price adjustments without completely altering your solution.

Immediately following proposal submission, begin preparing for customer questions (*please see note on next page*.) Make sure your contracts shop knows to notify you of any communications from the customer concerning the acquisition. Every response needs to consider what impact it has or may have on the proposal you submitted and any adjustments you may need to make later. Large acquisitions can go through multiple rounds of questions. Some questions are new, and some are follow-ups. You need to make sure your response doesn't contradict another answer or any aspect of your proposal. Often people selected to respond to a question on one area of a proposal are unaware of what is in other parts of the proposal or any interdependencies that may cut across them. Make sure you are involved in reviewing and responding to questions to prevent disconnects from happening. Another important point: DO NOT question the validity of an evaluation team question. Even if you think you have explained something clearly and succinctly, if they tell you they don't understand what you're trying to say, take their word for it.

Note: By questions, we mean any request from the customer for clarification, resubmission, or adjustment to your proposal. While these normally are part of formal discussions, they can also come about because of changes to the solicitation, a post-proposal submittal, or a variety of other unusual circumstances.

Chapter 23
Capture Management is Eternal

"Hurry – I think we're gaining on him!"

Make this your mantra and learn that capture continues, even though the activities change. If you don't keep working capture through award, you can lose opportunities to influence the outcome.

Staying on top of the relationships

Most of this book addresses what happens *before the solicitation drops*—connection with the client, stakeholders, and competitors; research; competitive analysis; price to win; staffing and teaming; and more. We cannot emphasize strongly enough: your job as capture manager doesn't stop when the proposal gets submitted, and neither does the need to maintain relationships. This includes your company's management, members of the capture team, teammates, and customers. You need to be the focal point for keeping the network alive. This doesn't need to be more than touching bases with folks every month or so to make sure you're keeping up to date. This is particularly important when the customer evaluation drags out over months, as it can. Folks tend to move on and focus on their new assignments. You want them still thinking about your opportunity and interested in re-engaging should you need them.

There are times when, even post award, you'll be included in future discussions on this and other opportunities if you have developed relationships. Never let a relationship drop!

Maintaining contact with the customer

"You aren't allowed to talk to the client!"
How often have you heard this refrain? Well, we're here to tell you that as an absolute, it's just WRONG! It's definitely true you aren't allowed to contact them or talk to them about the solicitation or the source selection. However, the modern world of communication provides you with many possibilities. You can continue to write blogs; attend and present at seminars, conferences, and workshops where your client might be; and continue to talk about work you may already be doing for them or other work they may care about. Be in the right place at the right time or have the right people there. Make sure you communicate not about the opportunity but about their areas of interest. Continuing relationships are important for future opportunities and just to maintain connections. Use these opportunities to keep your company's name and what you offer in front of your clients, customers, and prospects.

After award

First, get a debrief—win or lose. A debrief is especially useful as you prepare for your next capture. You want to learn what the evaluators considered strengths, significant strengths, weaknesses, significant weaknesses, and deficiencies. Remember if you're a loser, one of the customer's objectives during the evaluation debrief is to convince you there is no basis for a protest. They will emphasize shortcomings in your proposal and areas where the winner set themselves apart. Learn from these. Likewise, if you were the winner, learn from what they liked about your proposal, including whether it was easy to evaluate.

After the debrief, the cycle begins again. Win or lose, make sure to maintain your connections as you want to know how your company is perceived in the marketplace. You never know what else could crop up in the future!

If you have won, you should already be thinking about the recompete. Remember, we said capture never ends. Official capture for a recompete should begin 12 to 18 months after award. You need to identify:

- how to keep your customer happy and successful;
- what competitors might be interested in the follow-on;
- ways to ensure all contract options are exercised;
- new projects that will be ongoing during the next procurement cycle;
- steps to reduce cost (e.g., greening your staff) or improve efficiency (e.g., introducing technology); and
- books and training to keep customers happy and successfully manage projects.

Capture management is ETERNAL

Three Final Thoughts

1. Capture is a team sport. Done enthusiastically and done well it is fun, challenging, and highly collaborative.
2. While each of us has spent more than 40 years in the business world, we have all found winning government work is the most complicated. Tough competition. Moving targets. And almost an endless number of variables.
3. Doing everything we suggest in this book will improve your chances of winning. It doesn't guarantee a win. So, celebrate your wins. Learn from your losses. And give it your all.

Appendix

"Just remember what we taught you and you'll do fine!"

Appendices

SUGGESTED READING

Understanding How the Game Works

How to Play the Federal Contractor Game to Win by David Kritzer

More Solutions for Winning the Federal Contractor Game by David Kritzer

10 steps to creating high-scoring proposals by Bob Lohfeld

Positioning to Win by James M. Beveridge and Edward J. Velton

Successful Proposal Strategies for Small Businesses by Robert S. Frey

Managing Your Capture

High Performance Sales Organizations by Darlene M. Coker, Edward R. Del Gaizo, Kathleen A. Murray, and Sandra L. Edwards

The Checklist Manifesto: How to Get Things Right by Atul Gawande

https://blog.hubspot.com/marketing/psychological-biases-selling and other information posted on the Internet regarding this topic.

Improving Solutioning

Thinking Fast and Slow by Daniel Kahneman

Mobituaries: Great Lives Worth Reliving by Mo Rocca

Blink: The Power of Thinking Without Thinking by Malcolm Gladwell

Being More Convincing

The Storytelling Animal: How Stories Make Us Human by Jonathan Gottschall

Emotional Intelligence 2.0 by Travis Bradberry

To Sell is Human by Daniel Pink

Appendix

INFLUENCE MAP

	Engaged	Not Engaged
Strong Influence		
Weaker Influence		

Client

Decision Maker(s)

Competition

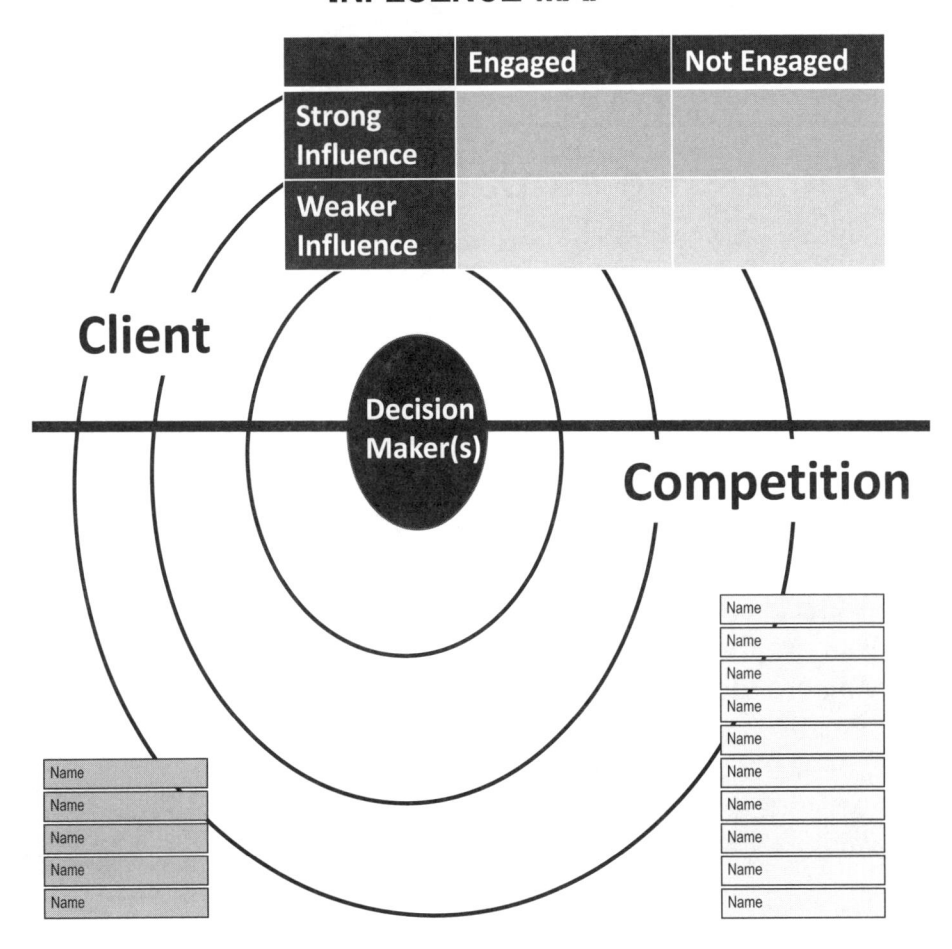

The influence map helps you identify who you need to know/talk to (client and competition) and then figure out how to get in front of them.

Depending on who it is, as part of this exercise, list their name and title, and identify their sphere of influence (e.g., procurement, management, client SME, advisor) and whether they know the company and/or individuals on the team. If so, their current perception and any potential negatives to overcome. This will help you prepare for your meetings. Remember, this is not one and done when working capture over months—revisit this, work this.

EMPATHY MAP CANVAS

Who are we empathizing with?
What do they do today?
What behavior have we observed?
What can we imagine them doing?

What do they HEAR?
What are they hearing others say?
What are they hearing from friends?
What are they hearing from colleagues?
What are they hearing second-hand?

What do they DO?
What do they do today?
What behavior have we observed?
What can we imagine them doing?

Pains
What are their fears, frustrations, and anxieties?

Appendix

What do they need to DO?
What do they need to do differently?
What jobs do they want to get done?
What decisions do they need to make?
How will we know they were successful?

What do they SEE?
What do they see in the marketplace?
What do they see in their immediate environment?
What do they see others saying and doing?

Gains
What are their wants, needs, hopes, and dreams?

What do they SAY?
What have we heard them say?
What can we imagine them saying?

Do the Empathy Map - Write to your client!

What does the customer
THINK & FEEL?
- What really counts
- Major perceptions
- Worries & aspirations

What does the customer
HEAR?
- What friends say
- What boss says
- What influencers say

What does the customer
SEE?
- Environment
- Friends
- What the market offers

What does the customer
SAY & DO?
- Attitude in public
- Appearance
- Behavior towards others

PAIN?
- Fears
- Frustrations
- Obstacles

GAIN?
- Wants/needs
- Measures of success
- Obstacles

About the Authors

Each of us, David Browder, Ricki Henschel, and David Kritzer, have more than 40 years of experience winning business, mostly for federal contractors. Joe Sutliff has been doodling on napkins for more than 40 years. For more information, here are our websites:

DavidBrowderGroup.com

RickiHenschel.com

DavidKritzer.com

JoeSutliff.com

Playing the Contractor Game to Win